OTHER BOOKS BY DONALD S. HEINTZELMAN:

The Hawks of New Jersey
A Guide to Northeastern Hawk Watching
Finding Birds in Trinidad and Tobago
Autumn Hawk Flights
A Guide to Eastern Hawk Watching
North American Ducks, Geese & Swans
Hawks and Owls of North America
A Guide to Hawk Watching in North America
A Manual for Bird Watching in the Americas
The Illustrated Bird Watcher's Dictionary
A World Guide to Whales, Dolphins, and Porpoises
The Birdwatcher's Activity Book
The Migration of Hawks
Wildlife Protectors Handbook

GUIDE TO
OWL WATCHING
IN NORTH AMERICA

Donald S. Heintzelman

DOVER PUBLICATIONS, INC.
NEW YORK

Endorsed by the Wildlife Information Center, Inc.

Copyright © 1984, 1992 by Donald S. Heintzelman.
All rights reserved under Pan American and International
Copyright Conventions.

Published in Canada by General Publishing Company, Ltd., 30
Lesmill Road, Don Mills, Toronto, Ontario.
Published in the United Kingdom by Constable and Company,
Ltd., 3 The Lanchesters, 162–164 Fulham Palace Road, London
W6 9ER.

This Dover edition, first published in 1992, is an unabridged,
slightly revised republication of the work first published by the
Winchester Press ("An Imprint of New Century Publishers,
Inc."), Piscataway, N.J., 1984. For this edition the author has
updated Appendixes 1 and 2 and the section "Suggested Reading."

Manufactured in the United States of America
Dover Publications, Inc., 31 East 2nd Street, Mineola, N.Y.
11501

Library of Congress Cataloging-in-Publication Data

Heintzelman, Donald S.
    Guide to owl watching in North America / Donald S.
Heintzelman.
        p.   cm.
    Originally published: Piscataway, N.J. : Winchester Press,
c1984.
    Includes bibliographical references (p.   ) and index.
    ISBN 0-486-27344-X
    1. Owls—North America. 2. Bird watching—North America.
I. Title.
QL696.S8H44 1992
598′.97′097—dc20   92-1742
                                                          CIP

To the memory of
Earl Lincoln Poole (1891–1972),
ornithologist, mammalogist, artist, and valued friend.

CONTENTS

Checklist of North American Owls   x

Preface   xi

Species Accounts   1
    Barn Owls: Tytonidae   1
    Typical Owls: Strigidae   3

Types and Methods of Owl Watching   27
    Diurnal Owl Watching   27
    Nocturnal Owl Watching   28
    Roosting Owls   32
    Nesting Owls   33
    Reading Sign   33
    Police Relations   34

Owl Watching Equipment   35
    Binoculars   35
    Telescope   35
    Tape Recorder   36
    Records   36
    Flashlight   36
    Pellet Bag   37
    Mammal Identification Guides   37
    Synoptic Skull Collection   38

Owl Pellets and Food Habits   39
    Pellets   39
    Food Habits   41

Owl Migrations and Invasions   43
    Seasonal Migrations   44
    Invasions   44

Survival Adaptations   47
    Vision   47
    Hearing   48
    Feathers   48
    Bills and Talons   49
    Size and Color   49

Owl Conservation   51
    Owl Nest Structures   51
    Additional Conservation Measures   54

Identification Plates and Field Marks   55

Owl Watching Sites   105

United States   106
    Arizona   106
    Arkansas   108
    California   109
    Colorado   112
    Connecticut   114
    Delaware   117
    Florida   118
    Georgia   120
    Idaho   121
    Illinois   122
    Indiana   123
    Iowa   124
    Kansas   125
    Kentucky   126
    Louisiana   127
    Maine   127
    Maryland   129
    Massachusetts   130
    Michigan   131
    Minnesota   132
    Mississippi   134
    Missouri   135
    Montana   138

Nebraska 138
New Jersey 139
New Mexico 140
New York 142
North Carolina 147
North Dakota 149
Ohio 149
Oklahoma 153
Oregon 154
Pennsylvania 155
Tennessee 161
Texas 162
Utah 166
Vermont 167
Virginia 168
Washington 168
Wisconsin 170

Canada 171
British Columbia 171
Manitoba 172
Newfoundland 173
Nova Scotia 174
Ontario 174
Quebec 176

Appendix 1: Accidental North American
Owl Sightings 181

Appendix 2: Owl Conservation Organizations 182

Appendix 3: Owl Pellet Data Form 186

Suggested Reading 187

Index 189

Checklist of North American Owls

( )   Common Barn Owl
( )   Eastern Screech Owl
( )   Western Screech Owl
( )   Whiskered Screech Owl
( )   Flammulated Owl
( )   Great Horned Owl
( )   Snowy Owl
( )   Northern Hawk Owl
( )   Northern Pygmy Owl
( )   Ferruginous Pygmy Owl
( )   Elf Owl
( )   Burrowing Owl
( )   Spotted Owl
( )   Barred Owl
( )   Great Gray Owl
( )   Long-eared Owl
( )   Short-eared Owl
( )   Boreal Owl
( )   Northern Saw-whet Owl

PREFACE

More than twenty-five years ago, I saw my first nestling Eastern Screech Owl and became fascinated by owls generally. Then followed field studies of nesting Great Horned Owls, Long-eared Owls, and roosting Northern Saw-whet Owls. Later, in the mid-1960s, as a graduate student at Lehigh University under ecologist F. J. Trembley, I spent months studying the distribution, population density, and certain ecological aspects of Common Barn Owls in parts of eastern Pennsylvania. Portions of that study were published in the Delaware Valley Ornithological Club's journal *Cassinia*. Then followed owl food habit studies and more general field observations of these predatory birds in a variety of locations in North America, the West Indies, South America, and Africa.

Today many more people are interested in owls—for research, conservation, and recreational birding purposes—than when I began looking at these birds. This book, however, is the first full-scale owl-watching field guide ever published, although I discussed various aspects of the subject earlier in two books—*Hawks and Owls of North America* and *A Manual for Bird Watching in the Americas*. I hope this guide will stimulate other people to study owls (perhaps even publish new information about them), take additional steps to augment owl conservation, and lead to new adventures in recreational owl watching. Perhaps the book also will stimulate others to invent new owl-watching and/or study techniques or possibly establish a special owl watching, study, and conservation organization on the order of the long defunct Hawk and Owl Society that was active during the 1930s.

During the preparation of this guide, a variety of books were consulted, including my own *Hawks and Owls of North America, A Guide to Hawk Watching in North America, A Manual for Bird Watching in the Americas,* and *North American Ducks, Geese & Swans,* as well as Austing and Holt's *The World of the Great Horned Owl,* Barbour's *Kentucky Birds: A Finding Guide,* Bent's *Life Histories of North American Birds of Prey* (Part 2), Bowman and Kale's *Where to Find Birds in Florida,* Burrow's *A Birdwatcher's Guide to Atlantic Canada,* Drennan's *Where to Find Birds in New York State,* Eckert's *A Birder's Guide to Minnesota,* Farrand's *The Audubon Society Master Guide to Birding,* Hammerstrom's *Birds of Prey of Wisconsin,* Harrison's *A Field Guide to Birds' Nests,* Karalus and Eckert's *The Owls of North America,* Keller, Keller, and Keller's *Indiana Birds and Their Haunts,* Kutac's *Texas Birds/Where They Are and How to Find Them,* Lane's *A Birder's Guide to Southern California* and *A Birder's Guide to Southeastern Arizona,* Lane and Chartier's *A Birder's Guide to Churchill,* Lane and Holt's *A Birder's Guide to Denver and Eastern Colorado,* Lane and Tveten's *A Birder's Guide to the Texas Coast,* Nero's *The Great Gray Owl,* Peterson's *A Field Guide to the Birds* and *A Field Guide to Western Birds,* Pettingill's *A Guide to Bird Finding East of the Mississippi* and *A Guide to Bird Finding West of the Mississippi,* Pierson and Pierson's *A Birder's Guide to the Coast of Maine,* Proctor's *25 Birding Areas in Connecticut,* Ramsey's *Birding Oregon,* Reilly's *The Audubon Illustrated Handbook of American Birds,* Robbins' *A Guide to Field Identification/Birds of North America,* Thomson's *Birding in Ohio,* Tyler and Phillips' *Owls by Day and Night,* Wahl and Paulson's *A Guide to Bird Finding in Washington,* and Walker's *The Book of Owls.*

Reference also was made to various periodicals, including *American Birds, Audubon Leader, Auk, Bird-Banding, Cassinia, Condor, EBBA News, Journal of Field Ornithology, Monographs of the Western Foundation of Vertebrate Zoology, Proceedings of the Western Foundation of Vertebrate Zoology, Raptor Research,* and the *Wilson Bulletin.*

Treatment of the various species in the Genus *Otus* is a very complex problem, and for the purposes of this book I followed the general ideas set forth by Joe T. Marshall, Jr. in his July 1967 monograph describing *Parallel Variation in North and Middle American Screech-Owls* published by the Western Foundation of Vertebrate Zoology. However, in order to further follow the American Ornithologists' Union in the Sixth Edition of its Check-List of the birds of North America, I have elevated the so-called *kennicottii* group of Screech Owls to species level in the form of the Western Screech Owl (*Otus kennicottii*) while retaining the eastern North American Screech Owls in the form of the Eastern Screech Owl (*Otus asio*).

Numerous people also provided helpful information used in the preparation of this book. These people included Fred C. Arnold, Alan Brady, Helen C. Cruickshank, James J. Dinsmore, June Ficker, Marty Floyd, David B. Freeland, Theodore R. Hake, Greg Hanisek, Otto Heck, Robert L. Hines, Jack Holcomb, David B. Johnson, Lloyd Kiff, Randy Korotev, Carl D. Marti, M. W. McIntosh, Fred Mears, Robert W. Nero, Mark Nyhof, Kenneth C. Parkes, Floyd L. Parks, Charles W. Smith, David Stirling, Keith B. Sutton, Peter Vickery, George J. Wallace, Charles Wonderly, James D. Wilson, Robert Witzeman, and Alan Wormington.

Photographs are an important part of this book and I used my own when possible. Additional photographs are credited in the text to the institution, organization, or individual who provided them. A special note of thanks is due each of these sources.

Donald S. Heintzelman
Allentown, Pa.

SPECIES ACCOUNTS

The native owls of North America are separated into two families—barn owls and typical owls. They range in size from smaller than a man's hand to large and powerful birds capable of killing skunks, rabbits, and other large prey. Rodents, however, form the bulk of the food items captured by many owl species. Some owls have "ear tufts" (feathers that have nothing to do with hearing) whereas others lack them. Most species are various shades of brown, but several are white or nearly so. Although a few species are diurnal or partly so in habits, most are nocturnal.

Barn Owls: Tytonidae

COMMON BARN OWL *Tyto alba*   Plate 1

Length: 14 to 20 inches (35.5 to 51 centimeters).
Wingspread: 43 to 47 inches (109 to 119 centimeters).
Field Recognition: The subspecies *T. a. pratincola,* of North America, is delicately colored with a distinctive heart-shaped face, long feathered legs and toes, and brown eyes. There are two color phases. *Adults (white phase)*—Pure white on the undersides or occasionally slightly flecked with browns and black. The upperparts are tawny or buffy. *Adults (orange phase)*—No white in the plumage. Tawny or buffy on the undersides and the upperparts. Eyes dark brown; bill ivory; talons grayish-black. *Immature*—Similar to the adults but with more down visible. *Chick*—Covered with fuzzy white,

Common Barn Owl nest and eggs.

then woolly buffy-white, down. There is no juvenile plumage.
Flight Style: Relatively swift, graceful, and light as it shifts from side to side rather than in a straight line.
Voice: Hisses, shrill screeches, sneezes, and snores. In all it is impressive, often hair-raising, and sometimes blood-curdling.
Nest: None constructed. Eggs deposited on the floors of barns, in openings in silos, towers, buildings, and other tall structures as well as in holes in trees, cliffs, quarries, banks, and similar places. Also accepts large bird boxes as nest sites.
Eggs: 5 to 7 (rarely 3 to 24) usually white but occasionally slightly yellowish or bluish. Incubation period is 30 to 34 days, often 33 days.
Food: Largely rodents such as *Microtus* voles, mice, and rats. Occasionally other small to medium-size mammals; small birds (rarely); snakes, lizards, and frogs; fish (rarely); crayfish; and large insects.
Habitat: Mostly open country in remote areas as well as in close proximity to (or even within) towns and cities. Not uncommon even within large cities. Farms and other agricultural areas are important habitats.

North American Distribution: Extreme southern Canada southward through the contiguous United States.

Typical Owls: Strigidae

EASTERN SCREECH OWL *Otus asio*
Plates 2, 3, 4

Length: 8.3 to 8.9 inches (20.9 to 22.5 centimeters).

Wingspread: 20.1 to 22.6 inches (50.9 to 57.3 centimeters).

Field Recognition: A small gray, or red, tufted owl separated into five subspecies which form the *asio* incipient species group in North America north of Mexico. Northern birds tend to be larger with coarser markings than southern birds. Bill yellow, greenish-yellow, pistachio, or turquoise (never black). Eyes yellow, pupils black. Legs and feet feathered. Talons ivory-grayish. *Adults (gray phase)*—Sexes similar. Gray birds (57% of *asio*, 37% of *floridanus*, 94% of *hasbroucki*, 87% of *maxwelliae*, and 98% of *mccallii*) with varying amounts of dark or black streaks on the underside and dark mottling above contrasting sharply with the overall gray plumage. *Adults (red phase)*—Sexes similar. Birds of the subspecies *O. a. asio*, of the eastern United States and southern Canada, show the distinctive and vivid red (39% of the population) marked with dark streaks on the underside and elsewhere on the body with birds in the Southeast somewhat smaller, darker, and with more abundant markings. *O. a. floridanus*, of peninsular Florida westward along the Gulf Coast to the Mississippi River mouth, is very small and deeper red (24% of the population) than *asio*. *O. a. hasbroucki*, of central Kansas, Oklahoma, central Texas and especially the Edwards Plateau, usually is medium sized and gray but has a rare red color phase (5% of the population) similar to eastern *asio* but more heavily marked. *O. a. maxwelliae*, restricted to the eastern slopes of the Rocky Mountains from southern Saskatchewan southward to northeastern Colorado, is larger than *asio* and the palest and least marked race with red birds being rare (7% of the population). Finally *O. a. mccallii*, of the Rio Grande valley from the river mouth to the Big Bend, is small and lacks a true red phase but rarely has intermediate red birds (2% of the population) although most *mccallii* are dark buffy gray with black ventral marks suggesting some Western Screech

Owls (*O. kennicottii*). *Juvenile (gray phase)*—Sexes similar. Mottled brown on the upperparts washed with deep gray and faint grayish-buff bars. Underparts dull white barred with buff. Wings and tail similar to the adults. *Juvenal (red phase)*—Similar to gray phase juveniles but rufous. *Chick*—Pure white down changing within a few days to a second dirty gray down.

Flight Style: Rapid, steady wingbeats with occasional brief glides. Hovers rarely.

Voice: Very variable depending upon subspecies, but in general trills or a whinny, barks, yips, and bill-snapping. Eastern *asio* uses a primary song suggesting a horse-like whinny descending at the end or a secondary song consisting of a quivering, mellow trill all on one pitch; *hasbroucki* produces a primary song with a short terminal vibrato unlike the voice of the Western Screech Owl (*O. kennicottii*) with a range nearby; and *mccallii* uses only an inflected cry lacking the terminal tremolo.

Nest: None constructed. The eggs are deposited in natural cavities in trees, old flicker holes, openings of buildings, hollow stumps, and bird boxes.

Eggs: 4 or 5 (rarely 2 to 9) pure white with a moderate gloss. Incubation period is 26 days.

Food: Small rodents, especially *Microtus* voles and *Peromyscus* mice, small birds, reptiles, amphibians, fish, and invertebrates. Occasionally fruits, berries, and other plant matter.

Habitat: Extremely variable, depending upon subspecies and location, but generally open woodland in close proximity to fields, meadows, old fields, fencerows, orchards (especially apple), wooded canyons, marshes, edges of running waterways (creeks, streams, rivers), open areas and parks in small and large towns and cities, and even yards. Eastern *asio* prefers woodland but often uses other areas including orchards, marshes, and parks in urban areas; *floridanus* prefers oak woodlands, willow thickets, and swamp forest; *hasbroucki* uses large live oaks (Edwards Plateau), oak mott, woodland, riparian mesquites, parks, and gardens; *maxwelliae* prefers cottonwood forests along rivers; and *mccallii* uses large groves with willows, mesquites, mesquite bosque, and oak mott.

North American Distribution: North of Mexico distributed widely from the eastern slopes of the Rocky Mountains eastward along extreme southern Canada to southern Maine then eastward to the Atlantic Ocean and southward to Florida and northeastern Mexico.

WESTERN SCREECH OWL *Otus kennicottii*
Plate 5

Length: 6.0 to 9.2 inches (15.2 to 23.4 centimeters).
Wingspread: 18.9 to 23.7 inches (48.0 to 60.1 centimeters).
Field Recognition: A small gray, or rarely reddish, tufted owl separated into five subspecies which form the *kennicottii* incipient species group in North America north of Mexico. The bill is black except in *A. k. bendirei* which has a greenish-gray bill similar to the Eastern Screech Owl (*O. asio*). Eyes yellow, pupils black. Legs and feet feathered. Talons ivory-grayish. Northern owls are larger and more coarsely marked than southern birds, and owls from arid areas tend toward paler coloration than birds from humid areas. *Adults*—Sexes similar. Birds of the subspecies *O. k. kennicottii*, of coastal Alaska (Juneau and Sitka) and British Columbia southward to coastal Oregon, generally are very large and gray (88% of the population), but there also is a rare red (deep brown) color phase (7% of the population). *O. k. aikeni*, of eastern California, Nevada, Utah, southeastern Colorado, extreme western Oklahoma, Arizona, and New Mexico southward into Mexico, is medium in size and the palest gray of all Western Screech Owls. *O. k. bendirei*, of eastern Washington and Oregon, western Idaho, and southwestern Montana, is the largest of the races of Western Screech Owls, has a unique greenish-gray (not black) bill, is plain brown with "salt and pepper" dots above and wide streaks below, and has an intermediate red color phase (11% of the northern population). *O. k. suttoni*, of the Big Bend area of Texas westward to Guadalupe Canyon in Arizona and southward into Mexico, is the blackest of the races of the Western Screech Owl and a small bird. Finally *O. k. yumanensis*, of California's Colorado Desert and the lower Colorado River valley southward into Mexico, is small and pale-pinkish gray in color. *Juvenal*—Generally similar to the adults but perhaps less well marked.

Chick—Pure white down changing within a few days to a second dirty gray down.

Flight Style: Rapid, steady wingbeats with occasional brief glides. Hovers rarely.

Voice: Variable according to which subspecies is heard, but generally the primary song is a distinctive and mellow, pure pitch and tone, bouncing ball sound whereas the secondary song is a rapid double trill. The race *aikeni* uses a short primary song, *bendirei* uses a long primary song, *kennicottii* produces a long primary song ending with a beautiful roll, *suttoni* uses a short primary song, and *yumanensis* also uses a short primary song.

Nest: None constructed. The eggs are deposited in natural cavities in trees, old woodpecker holes, openings in buildings, hollow stumps, and bird boxes.

Eggs: 4 or 5 (rarely 2 to 9) pure white with a moderate gloss. Incubation period is 26 days.

Food: Small rodents, *Microtus* voles and other small rodents, small birds, small reptiles and amphibians, fish, and various invertebrates.

Habitats: Variable depending upon which subspecies is considered, but generally open woodland, desert oases, riparian woodland, and even parks and open areas with adequate trees in towns and cities. The subspecies *aikeni* tends to use cottonwood forest, groves of mesquite, hackberry, and other vegetation, palo verde-saguaro woods in deserts, open oak woodland in foothills, and riparian groves of sycamores even up to elevations of 5,500 feet; *bendirei* uses riparian groves in open ponderosa pine forest, oak woodland, blue oak-differ pine woodland, riparian woods along streams, and suburban shade trees; *kennicottii* uses oak woodland and Douglas fir forest that is low and dense and riparian woodland along streams passing through lowland forest; *suttoni* uses woodland of piñon and oak in the high Chisos Mountains in Texas, but mesquite and willow thickets along the Rio Grande River; and *yumanensis* tends to prefer thick willow stands and tamarisk stands growing along the lower Colorado River and riparian oases in the Colorado Desert in California.

North American Distribution: Western North America from the Pacific coast of Alaska and Canada southward into Mexico and eastward to the western slopes of the Rocky Mountains.

WHISKERED SCREECH OWL *Otus trichopsis*
Plate 6

Length: 6.6 to 7.5 inches (16.7 to 19.0 centimeters).
Wingspread: 14.8 to 20.8 inches (37.5 to 52.8 centimeters).
Field Recognition: A small light gray tufted owl, similar to
the Western Screech Owl and formerly known as the Spotted
Screech Owl, but intermediate in size between Western
Screech and Flammulated Owls. It differs also from other
Otus species in voice, habitat requirements, and geographic
range. Sexes similar. Eyes yellow and pupils black. Bill pale
yellowish-green to greenish-gray. Talons slaty-gray to black.
Adults—In the subspecies *O. t. aspersus*, of the 4,000 to 6,500
foot elevation of the Chiricahua and Huachuca Mountains of
southeastern Arizona, the birds are light gray with ventral
crossbars and broad black marks on the shafts. The feathers
on the face exhibit exceptionally bristly tips producing the
impression of whiskers from which the species derives its
name. Other subspecies farther south in Mexico also exhibit a
distinctive red color phase lacking in Arizona birds. *Juvenal*—
Dull grayish-brown on the uppersides with faint grayish-
white mottling and bars. Undersides dusky white with broad
slate-brown bars. *Chick*—Information unavailable.
Flight Style: Hunts with short and straight flight to other
branches or to the ground then back to the perch. Occasionally flutters in the tops of trees.
Voice: Distinctive and the only means of separating this
species from the Western Screech Owl. The primary or
territorial song consists of 8 or 9 short, evenly pitched *boot-
boot-boot-boot-boot-boot-boot-boot* notes. The secondary or
duetting song is a two part, Morse Code-like series of evenly
pitched notes beginning with two short notes followed by
three longer notes. The sequence is given three times without
a pause, the end of the last sequence also having an added
longer note.
Nest: Cavities in trees or abandoned woodpecker holes in
large white oak tree branches (rather than trunks); also uses
nest boxes.
Eggs: 3 or 4, white without gloss. Incubation period unknown.
Food: Hunts among the foliage and branches in dense groves
in canyons and mountain slopes. Insects (especially winged

species) including short-horned and long-horned grasshoppers, field crickets, roaches, praying mantis, leafhoppers, beetles, moths and their larvae, flying ants, and bees; also centipedes, spiders, and rarely small rodents and small birds. **Habitat:** Steep, north-facing mountainsides and shady, narrow canyons with dense groves of oaks within pine-oak woodland at elevations between 4,000 and 7,000 feet. **North American Distribution:** Mountains of southeastern Arizona.

FLAMMULATED OWL *Otus flammeolus*
Plate 6

Length: 5.9 to 7.4 inches (14.9 to 18.7 centimeters).
Wingspread: 14.9 to 18.2 inches (37.8 to 46.2 centimeters).
Field Recognition: *Adult*—A rare, local, and very small tufted owl (smallest species in the genus *Otus*) ranging in color from pure gray to grayish-rufous to reddish but lacking distinctive color phases. Ventral crossbars always are present and reddish birds are very well marked with black. The tiny ear tufts are not longer than surrounding head feathers. The irises are distinctive in being dark brown (not yellow). It is represented in North America by the subspecies *O. f. flammeolus. Juvenal*—Similar to adults, but with coarser and more regular barring on the back. *Chick*—Covered with snowy white down.
Flight Style: Darting, sometimes jerky, with some hovering. Glides occasionally.
Voice: *Male*—A low pitched, resonant hoot occasionally preceded by one or two still lower grace-notes. *Female*— Unlike the male's song. A higher pitched whinny or quiver.
Nest: An old woodpecker hole in a pine, oak, or aspen tree. Does not appear to use nest boxes.
Eggs: 3 or 4 (rarely 2 to 5), white with a slight gloss and very finely granulated. Incubation period estimated at about 25 days.
Food: Entirely insectivorous with moths, beetles, and grasshoppers forming a large proportion of the diet but a variety of other insects also taken occasionally. Rarely takes millipedes, centipedes, scorpions, and spiders.
Habitat: Open pine forests with brush-like understory in the

western United States at mountain elevations between 4,500 and 10,000 feet.

North American Distribution: Summers locally from southern British Columbia southward through the mountains of Washington, Oregon, California, Nevada, Arizona, and Texas into Mexico. Migrates south of the United States and winters in Mexico, but a few birds may also occur in winter in extreme southern California.

GREAT HORNED OWL *Bubo virginianus*
Plates 7, 8

Length: 18.4 to 25.7 inches (46.7 to 65.2 centimeters).
Wingspread: 49 to 62.1 inches (124.4 to 157.7 centimeters).
Field Recognition: A very large, powerful, and aggressive owl separated into at least 10 subspecies in North America. The birds exhibit great variation in color and size, but essentially are largely brown and extensively barred on the underparts. Above they are darker brown, with the darkest areas appearing on the top of the head and back. A white throat, or bib, is distinctive. The bird appears almost neckless, and the head is large. Females are about one-third larger than males. *Adults (both sexes)*—A typical individual of the subspecies *B. v. virginianus*, of the eastern half of the contiguous United States and extreme southern Canada, is medium brown with darker brown and black spots on the upperparts and wings. The underparts are lighter with fine dark brown or black bars. The bib (upper breast and lower throat) is white, and the eye discs are reddish bordered on the outer edges with black. The eyebrows exhibit only a touch of white compared with some subspecies. Eyes yellow with black pupils. Bill and talons black. *B. v. pallescens*, of the Southwest, is similar to eastern *virginianus* but somewhat paler whereas *B. v. wapacuthu* of most of western and southern Canada is extremely pale (sometimes almost white). In contrast, *B. v. saturatus* of Pacific Northwest forests is extremely dark brown with a bold white throat and bib and whitish eyebrows. *B. v. heterocnemis*, of much of Quebec, Labrador, and Newfoundland, is large and dark but paler than *saturatus* on the underparts. *B. v. pacificus*, of most of California, is somewhat smaller and darker than *pallescens*. *B. v. occi-*

Great Horned Owl nest and eggs.

dentalis, of the Northwest, is darker and larger than *pallescens.*
B. v. algistus, of coastal Alaska, is darker on the upperparts and
not as heavily barred below compared with *occidentalis* and
larger than *pacificus. B. v. lagophonus,* of inland Alaska,
British Columbia, and parts of Washington, Oregon, Idaho,
and Montana, suggests *saturatus* but is somewhat lighter.
Other subspecies have been described but are not recognized currently. *Juvenal (sexes similar)*—Similar to the adults
on the wings and tail but the ear tufts are shorter, the bib is
duller and smaller, there is some down remaining on the
birds, and the overall appearance of the plumage is ruddier
than in adults. The pupils of birds still in the nest are blue
rather than black as in adults, but the irises are yellow.
Chick—Covered with pure white down followed by dirty,
buff-colored down.
Flight Style: Heavy flight generally not above the tops of
trees, but occasionally soars to high altitudes. More commonly
soars not far above the ground for brief periods of time.
Voice: A varied assortment of hoots, screams, hisses, whistles,
and shrieks. The deep, resonant hoot that is best known is
audible for several miles and is a foghorn-like *whooo-whooo*

whooooooo whooo-whoooo. Sometimes other vocalizations also are used.

Nest: Generally an abandoned hawk (frequently Red-tailed Hawk), eagle, crow, or heron nest. Occasionally natural hollows in trees, hollow logs, openings in cliffs, silos, and nest boxes.

Eggs: 2 or 3 (rarely 1 to 6), dull white sometimes touched with yellow or bluish. Incubation period estimated between 28 and 35 days.

Food: Extremely varied throughout its extensive geographic range, but generally medium-size mammals (rats, hares, rabbits), birds, reptiles, amphibians, fish, and invertebrates.

Habitat: Dense forests, large woodlots, extensive tracts of wilderness, open woodland, cypress hammocks, marshes in close proximity to woodland, canyons, cliffs, and river valleys.

North American Distribution: Northern Alaska and Canada southward throughout the contiguous United States.

SNOWY OWL *Nyctea scandiaca*   Plate 9

Length: 20.9 to 30.2 inches (53.1 to 76.7 centimeters).

Wingspread: 51.9 to 71.6 inches (131.8 to 181.8 centimeters).

Field Recognition: A large, spectacular, and distinctive Arctic owl with white plumage and yellow eyes. *Adult (male)*—Pure white, or nearly so, with limited slaty spots on the back and the tips of the wings and tail. Legs feathered to the toes. Eyes bright yellow with black pupils. Bill and talons black. *Adult (female)*—Similar to the adult male but larger and with more body markings consisting mostly of heavy brownish spots on the upperparts and bars on the undersides. *Juvenal (sexes similar)*—Dusky brown or sooty-gray with much bolder spots and bars than in the adult plumage. The juvenal plumage is retained for up to 14 months. *Chick*— Covered with pure white down soon replaced with long, thick, fluffy, dark gray down.

Flight Style: Strong, steady, and direct much like a falcon's but slower. The body appears to undulate while the bird is in flight. The head also tends to turn back and forth as the bird remains in the air.

Voice: A booming *whoo whoo whoo whoo* that carries for long distances over the tundra. Other calls also are used occasionally. Generally, however, the birds remain silent.

Nest: A shallow scrape or depression on top of an elevated mound. Limited vegetation and feathers sometimes line the depression. On very rare occasions abandoned eagle nests in trees are used, and nests also have been reported placed on gravel banks.

Eggs: 5 to 8 (rarely 3 to 13) white to creamy-white but quickly becoming soiled. Incubation period estimated at 32 to 33 days.

Food: Lemmings and mice form much of the diet in the Arctic, but a varied assortment of other small and medium-size mammals and birds also are taken.

Habitat: Tundra during the summer; in winter, south of the Arctic, often along coastlines, shorelines of large lakes, open fields and pastures, and marshland.

North American Distribution: Virtually all of Alaska and Canada southward into extreme upstate New England and the Great Lakes states. During invasion years sometimes wanders farther southward.

NORTHERN HAWK OWL *Surnia ulula*
Plate 10

Length: 14.3 to 17.6 inches (36.3 to 44.7 centimeters).

Wingspread: 30.6 to 35.1 inches (77.7 to 89.1 centimeters).

Field Recognition: An unusual hawk-like, medium-size, slim, rich brown northern owl flecked with white spots and bars. It is noted for its unusual diurnal habits. In North America it is represented by the subspecies *S. u. caparoch*. Because of its erect posture when sitting, and long tail, it suggests to some degree an American Kestrel's shape but is larger. *Adults (sexes similar)*—Dark brown on the upperparts flecked with white spots on the scapulars, neck, and head. The facial disc is whitish with a black outer rim. Chin dark, throat white, and underparts white with numerous dark brown bars. The tail is brown with 7 or 8 narrow, broken white bands; the tip is buffy. Eyes bright yellow, pupils black. Bill and talons black. *Juvenal*—Similar to the adult but with less spotting on the upperparts, the undersides more chestnut-brown, and the tail with a broader whitish tip. *Chick*—Probably covered with white down but subject to field study.

Flight Style: Falcon-like with rapid, erratic wingbeats in a direct line not unlike that of a Peregrine Falcon. Hovers occasionally like an American Kestrel. In woodland the flight becomes accipiter-like.

Voice: Varied but typically a chattering *kikikikiki* or a high-pitched *wita-wita-wita.* Other vocalizations also are reported. All in all, more hawk-like than owl-like.

Nest: Cavities in the tops of broken-off trees, occasionally old Pileated Woodpecker holes or other natural hollows in trees, abandoned hawk or crow nests, or badly constructed platforms of twigs lined with bits of vegetation and some tufts of down from the birds.

Eggs: 3 to 7 (rarely 2 to 9), pure white (rarely yellowish) with a slight gloss. Incubation period is about 25 days.

Food: Lemmings, and other small rodents, along with some medium-size mammals, form the bulk of the summer diet. In winter, ptarmigan are important prey supplemented by grouse, hare, and mice.

Habitat: Tamarack swamp and boreal forest fringe, especially where dead trees occur in some numbers. Also mixed hardwood forests in some areas. Often its habitat exhibits a brush character.

North American Distribution: Much of Alaska and Canada southward into New England and the northern Great Lakes states. Sometimes ventures farther southward in winter.

NORTHERN PYGMY OWL *Glaucidium gnoma*
Plate 11

Length: 6.3 to 7.5 inches (16 to 19 centimeters).

Wingspread: 14.5 to 15.8 inches (36.8 to 40.1 centimeters).

Field Recognition: A small, bold, aggressive, mostly diurnal, tuftless Western owl noted for holding its long tail at an angle, black streaks on the flanks, and a black patch on each side of the back of the neck. Four subspecies are represented in North America. *Adult male (gray phase)*—A typical individual of the subspecies *G. g. californicum* of British Columbia southward through the Rocky Mountains and eastern Washington, Oregon, and California, has the uppersides dark slaty-brown spotted with white, head with numerous white spots, eyebrows white, underparts white with dark brown streaking, and tail dark brownish-black with narrow white bands. Eyes yellow with black pupils. Bill greenish-yellow, talons grayish-black. *Adult male (red phase)*—Similar to gray phase birds but nearly chestnut in color rather than slaty brown. *Adult female* *(red phase)*—Similar to the male, but larger and usually more reddish in color. *G. g. gnoma*, of the southeastern corner of Arizona (Atasco, Chiricahua, Huachuca, Pajarito, and Santa Rita mountains) southward into Mexico, is similar to *G. g. californicum* but smaller. *G. g. grinnelli*, restricted to a narrow coastal strip from northern British Columbia southward to central California, has its upperparts nearly blackish-brown unlike other North American subspecies of this owl and in its woodpecker-like flight keeps its tail spread unlike other subspecies. *G. g. swarthi*, generally restricted to Vancouver Island, British Columbia, is darker and smaller than *G. g. californicum* and also tends to be much more shy and reclusive than any of the other North American subspecies of this owl. *Juvenal (both sexes)*—Similar to adults but generally lacking the spots exhibited by adults. *Chick*—Information unavailable.

Flight Style: Short flights above the ground with rapid wingbeats sometimes suggesting a shrike or an American Kestrel.

Voice: A mellow, dove-like *oooo* uttered every couple of seconds; also *poook poook poook pook pook*. Other calls also are used at times.

Nest: Abandoned holes of small to medium-size woodpeckers. The owls sometimes use such sites for several successive years.

Eggs: 4 (rarely 3 to 6) white to slightly creamy-white usually without a gloss. Incubation period estimated at about 22 days.

Food: Birds and mammals (often much larger than the owl), reptiles, amphibians, insects, spiders, scorpions, and centipedes.

Habitat: Mixed or coniferous woodland with openings, and wooded canyons; commonly hunts over grassland and meadows in proximity to woodland.

North American Distribution: From southeastern Alaska, British Columbia, and Alberta southward through the Pacific West and Rockies to Mexico.

FERRUGINOUS PYGMY OWL *Glaucidium brasilianum*   Plate 12

Length: 5.8 to 7.2 inches (14.7 to 18.2 centimeters).
Wingspread: 14.3 to 16 inches (36.3 to 40.6 centimeters).
Field Recognition: A small, relatively uncommon, rusty-

backed owl of the Southwest. The subspecies *G. b. cactorum* is represented in North America. It can be confused with the similar Northern Pygmy Owl, but the back of the Ferruginous Owl is rusty and unmarked. *Adults (red phase)*—Reddish except on the tail which is reddish-gray with black bands. The back is rusty and lacks the markings distinctive of the related Northern Pygmy Owl. The undersides, especially the breast, have brownish (not black) streaks. Females are slightly larger than males. *Adults (gray phase)*—Upperparts gray with a brownish cast; tail slaty-gray with black bands. *Juvenal*—Like the adults but without crown markings. *Chick*—Information unavailable.

Flight Style: Direct and slightly undulating with rapid wingbeats and almost no gliding.

Voice: A series of *chuk* sounds made 2 to 3 times each second.

Nest: In old holes of woodpeckers in cacti, cottonwood trees, or mesquite.

Eggs: 3 or 4 (rarely 5) white. Incubation period not determined.

Food: Birds, mammals, insects, reptiles, amphibians, and invertebrates.

Habitat: Deserts, especially with saguaro and cholla cacti, but also areas with wooded creeks and mesquite thickets.

North American Distribution: Confined to southern Arizona and eastward to the lower Rio Grande Valley in Texas.

ELF OWL *Micrathene whitneyi* Plate 12

Length: 5.3 to 6.6 inches (13.4 to 16.7 centimeters).

Wingspread: 13.9 to 15.1 inches (35.3 to 38.3 centimeters).

Field Recognition: A tiny southwestern owl (smallest in North America) without ear tufts. *Adults (gray phase)*—*M. w. whitneyi,* of much of the Southwest, is grayish-brown on the uppersides marked irregularly with small buffy spots, a black-and-white shoulder line, spotted crown, white eyebrows, buffy facial discs, and buffy-reddish throat. Undersides buffy with dusky bars, tail with 4 or 5 narrow buffy bands. Eyes yellow with black pupils. Legs and feet very lightly feathered with the feet appearing almost naked. Bill and talons grayish-black. Individuals of the subspecies *M. w. idonea,* of the lower Rio Grande Valley of Texas, is grayer with whiter whites than *M. w. whitneyi. Adults (brown phase)*—Similar to gray phase individuals but darker brownish, especially on the back. *Juvenal*—Similar to adults but without crown spots, facial discs darker than in adults, and the undersides grayish with narrow gray bars. *Chick*—Covered with pure white down.

Flight Style: Swiftly with rapid wingbeats.

Voice: A low *churp.* Also a yipping *whi-whi-whi-whi-whi-whi* or *chewk-chewk-chewk-chewk.*

Nest: A woodpecker hole in a hardwood tree or saguaro cactus.

Eggs: 3 or 4 (rarely 2 to 5), white with a moderate gloss. Incubation period is 14 days.

Food: Insects, spiders, scorpions, and centipedes. Also shrews, small mice, and small birds.

Habitat: Generally low, arid, desert with mesquite, cacti, and creosote bush; also canyons, ravines, and grassland at higher elevations up to 7,000 feet.

North American Distribution: The extreme Southwest from the lower Rio Grande Valley in Texas westward through extreme southern New Mexico and Arizona to extreme southeastern California.

BURROWING OWL *Athene cunicularia*
Plate 13

Length: 8.4 to 11.2 inches (21.3 to 28.4 centimeters).

Wingspread: 22 to 24.3 inches (55.8 to 61.7 centimeters).

Field Recognition: A small, brown, tuftless, diurnal ground dwelling owl with white eyebrows and throat, a black throat band, and long legs. *Adults (sexes similar)*—A typical individual of the western North American subspecies *A. c. hypugaea* is brown on the uppersides marked with buffy spots, round-headed with frequent head-bobbing, has whitish eyebrows and sandy-buff facial discs. The undersides are brownish-buffy marked with light spots. The brownish tail has 4 to 6 narrow, irregular, buffy bands and a buffy-white terminal band. The long legs are feathered but otherwise are unmarked and suggest, to some extent, the long legs of a Barn Owl. Eyes bright yellow with black pupils. Bill grayish-yellow, talons grayish-black. Individuals of the Florida subspecies, *A. c. floridana,* are darker than *hypugaea* on the uppersides and have shorter and less feathered legs. *Juvenal*—Similar to adults but without spots on the buffy-grayish crown, hindneck, and back. The undersides are unmarked, and the throat band is dark brown. *Chick*—Covered scantily with grayish-white down changing to the juvenal plumage when the nestling is roughly one-half grown.

Flight Style: Suggests that of the American Kestrel, with labored wingbeats, generally close to the ground, and lands in a manner similar to that of the woodcock. Often hovers when hunting. Also uses combinations of glides and rapid wing-beats.

Voice: A *cack-cack-cack-cack* alarm note, and a cooing *twut twut twut* courtship note.

Nest: In underground chambers of prairie dogs, or in burrows excavated by the owl itself. Generally a mound of soil outside the burrow entrance provides a lookout perch for the birds.

Eggs: 7 to 9 (rarely 6 to 12), white with a faint bluish tinge. Incubation period is 28 to 29 days.

Food: A varied assortment of insects, scorpions, centipedes, other invertebrates, fish, reptiles, amphibians, small mammals, and birds. Also fruits and seeds.

Habitat: Unbroken prairies and plains, airports, farms, deserts, dikes, and similar locations.

North American Distribution: In the West from the southern portions of the western Canadian provinces southward through the western United States into Mexico; also in Central and southern Florida. The species is expanding its range in Florida.

SPOTTED OWL *Strix occidentalis*   Plate 14

Length: 15.3 to 23.9 inches (38.8 to 60.7 centimeters).
Wingspread: 37.1 to 44.5 inches (94.2 to 113 centimeters).
Field Recognition: A rare western North American counter-part of the Barred Owl of the East. The markings on the underside of the Spotted Owl are horizontal (vertical in the Barred Owl). *Adults (sexes similar)*—An example of *S. o. occidentalis*, of interior California, is round-headed and brown, like a Barred Owl, but differs from that species by being spotted with white on the breast and belly. Some individuals also have a white throat patch, and the eyebrows and lores also are white shading to buffy. The cinnamon-buffy facial discs are large with narrow reddish-brown semicircles extending outward from the eyes. Eyes brown; bill yellow;

talons blackish-gray. The subspecies *S. o. caurina,* of the Pacific Coast from southern British Columbia southward to central California, is darker than the other races of this species. *S. o. lucida,* of the Southwest southward into Mexico, is smaller than the other races, darker than *occidentalis,* but lighter than *caurina. Juvenal*—Suggests the first winter adult with buffy or ivory (not white) spots. *Chick*—Covered with gray down.

Flight Style: Buoyant but with heavy wingbeats.

Voice: A group of 3 *hoo hoo-hoo* notes, or a group of 4 *hoo who-who-whooo* notes. Some of the calls suggest a dog's barking.

Nest: Hollow tree trunks, deserted hawk or raven nests, potholes, and caverns on cliffs.

Eggs: 2 (rarely 3 or 4) white and slightly granulated. Incubation period estimated at 25 to 28 days.

Food: Rodents, small birds, and garbage and offal.

Habitat: Heavily wooded old-growth areas with rocky canyons and ravines.

North American Distribution: Western North America from southern British Columbia southward in a narrow belt into the Southwest and Mexico.

BARRED OWL *Strix varia*   Plate 15

Length: 16.1 to 24.2 inches (40.8 to 61.4 centimeters).

Wingspread: 38 to 50 inches (96.5 to 127 centimeters).

Field Recognition: A large wet or swampy woodland owl with a round head but without ear tufts. The breast is barred crosswise and the belly is streaked lengthwise—both good field marks. The birds sometimes hunt during the day. *Adults (sexes similar)*—The subspecies *S. v. varia* of much of the eastern United States and southern Canada, exclusive of the Southeast, is more or less typical by being grayish-brown with large facial discs, and *brown eyes.* Bill yellow; talons blackish-gray. The subspecies *S. v. georgica,* of the Southeast, is similar to *varia* but much darker in overall color; *S. v. helveola,* of southcentral Texas, is more reddish-brown than grayish-brown and is smaller than *varia. Juvenal*—Similar to the adult but with broad, buffy-white barring on the underparts, and darker brown barring on the back, scapulars, and wing coverts. *Chicks*—Covered with soft, thick, silky white down.

A second down develops when the chick is between two and three weeks old.

Flight Style: Buoyant and light but with slow, heavy wing-beats. Rarely soars, but frequently flies high and always silently.

Voice: Loud and very vocal hooting, often in response to each other. Sometimes a rhythmic *hoo-hoo-to-hoo-oo, hoo-hoo-hoo-to-whoo-oo,* or a *hoohoo-hoo-hoo-hoo-hoo-hoo-hooaw* repeated twice. Suggests "who cooks for you? who cooks for you all?" in English.

Nest: Frequently uses abandoned Red-shouldered Hawk or crow nests; also large, deep hollows in trees.

Eggs: 2 or 3 (rarely 4 or 5), white with a slightly rough texture. Incubation period is about 28 days.

Food: A varied assortment of small to medium-size mammals and birds in addition to reptiles, amphibians, fish, and insects.

Habitat: Extensive forests, heavily wooded swamps, and other dark wooded tracts. Frequently hunts over nearby farmland, open country, and sometimes even in villages, towns, and cities.

North American Distribution: Widely throughout the eastern two-thirds of the contiguous United States and southern Canada.

GREAT GRAY OWL *Strix nebulosa*
Plates 16, 17

Length: 24.3 to 33.3 inches (61.7 to 84.5 centimeters).
Wingspread: 51.4 to 60.1 inches (130.5 to 152.6 centimeters).
Field Recognition: Spectacular and markedly diurnal. The largest of the North American owls represented on the continent by the subspecies *S. n. nebulosa. Adult (male)*— Brownish or beige with dense, fluffy plumage, a very large round head, no ear tufts, large "flattened" facial discs marked with five (usually) concentric semicircles, and a black chin spot with a distinctive white chin stripe on each side. The white chin stripes can be seen even in very dim light. The undersides are marked with lengthwise stripes. Tail very long, often very worn in females, and paler than the coloration of the body feathers, with numerous irregular bands. Legs feathered to the toes. Eyes yellow. Bill large, varying from ivory to pale olive-green to bright yellow. Talons blackish.

Adult (female)—Similar to the male but considerably larger. *Juvenal*—Similar to, but uniformly grayer than adults. *Chick*—Covered with buffy-white down.

Flight Style: Slow and measured, generally only for short distances as between perches, and usually not very far above the ground.

Voice: A soft, mellow *Whoop!* or hoot; a booming *whooo-ooo-ooo-ooo*, deep in tone, repeated about three times; or a whinny suggesting a Screech Owl. Nesting females sometimes call *Sher-rick!* or an extended *Shreek!* Other calls also are known.

Nest: Abandoned hawk, raven, or crow nests placed at varying elevations in spruce or poplars, or rarely hawk nests on rocky walls. Also uses artificial nests provided for their use in some instances.

Eggs: 2 or 3 (rarely 4 or 5) dull white. Incubation period is 28 to 30 days, generally by the female.

Food: Voles (especially *Microtus* and *Clethrionomys*), moles, Red Squirrels, pocket gophers, and other smaller mammals. Birds are taken only rarely.

Habitat: Stunted transition forest (in the Hudson Bay Lowlands) to montane and subalpine forests from Alaska to California and Wyoming. Especially islands of tamarack or larch within spruce forests, or mature poplar stands adjacent to muskeg country. During southward winter invasions sometimes found in villages, towns, and cities where they perch on TV antennas, telephone poles, fence posts, barns, houses, and other structures.

North American Distribution: Alaska and western Canada southward into California and the Rocky Mountains of the contiguous United States and eastward in southern Canada's boreal forests. During rare winter invasions farther southward into the extreme northern United States.

LONG-EARED OWL *Asio otus*   Plates 18, 19

Length: 13 to 16.1 inches (33 to 40.8 centimeters).
Wingspread: 36.3 to 43.3 inches (92.2 to 109.9 centimeters).
Field Recognition: A widely distributed, slender, owl with ear tufts closer toward the center of the crown than in the horned owl and lengthwise streaks on the undersides. Frequently seen roosting in a conifer or deciduous tree, near the trunk, in a somewhat elongated posture. *Adult (male)*—A

typical individual of the subspecies *A. o. wilsonianus*, of much of southern Canada and the contiguous United States exclusive of the West, is mottled slaty-brown to grayish-white on the upperparts and lighter on the undersides with dark lengthwise streaks. The long, narrow ear tufts have considerable black present. The face has whitish eyebrows and orange-brown facial discs marked with black edges. Eyes yellow with black pupils; bill blackish; talons slaty-black. *A. o. tuftsi*, of the West, is generally paler than Eastern birds. *Adult (female)*—Similar to the male but larger and somewhat paler. *Juvenal*—Similar to the adults but with darker cinnamon-red facial discs, smaller ear tufts, and black eyebrows. *Chick*—Sparingly covered with short, white down replaced in about 21 days with a grayish second down.

Flight Style: Noiseless, buoyant, and light. Hovers occasionally in butterfly-like manner; also glides occasionally.

Voice: Varied, but often a soft, hooting *quoo-quoo-quoo,* a prolonged *quoo-oo-oo,* or a soft *whoof-whoof-whoof.* Frequently snaps its bill near the nest where it also makes doglike and cat-like sounds.

Nest: Usually an old squirrel, crow, or hawk nest placed well aloft in a tree (generally a conifer) but occasionally low or even on the ground. On rare occasions in hollow tree stumps.

Eggs: 4 or 5 (rarely 3 to 8) white, smooth, and somewhat glossy. Incubation period 21 days, mostly (perhaps entirely) by the female.

Food: Rodents, shrews, and other small mammals; occasionally some birds, snakes, frogs, and insects.

Habitat: Frequently dense coniferous woodland, sometimes deciduous woodland, river woodland, woodlots, parks, and orchards.

North American Distribution: Central Canada southward through the contiguous United States.

SHORT-EARED OWL *Asio flammeus*
Plates 20, 21

Length: 13.3 to 17.1 inches (33.7 to 43.4 centimeters).
Wingspread: 38.3 to 44.1 inches (97.2 to 112 centimeters).
Field Recognition: An almost cosmopolitan, medium-size, diurnal owl represented in North America by the subspecies *A. f. flammeus.* It sometimes is observed hunting over fields and marshes during the day or at dawn or dusk. The ear tufts

Short-eared Owl nest and eggs.

Short-eared Owl winter habitat in New York State.

are barely visible even under ideal conditions. There are small, black, oblong patches on the undersides of the primaries at the base, and a creamy-brown wing patch on the upper surface. *Adult male (brown phase)*—Buffy-brown with dark streaks on the body, tiny ear tufts (not always visible), white eyebrows, throat, and chin, black eye circles, and buffy-brown facial discs outlined with semicircular white and black outer edges. Eyes bright yellow, pupils black. Bill and talons black. *Adult female (brown phase)*—Similar to the male but slightly larger and darker in color. *Adult male (gray phase)*—Similar to the brown phase but whitish or creamy-white with gray instead of brown markings. *Adult female (gray phase)*—Similar to the male but slightly larger and darker in color. *Juvenal*—Dark brown on the uppersides, orange-buff to gray below, with brownish-black facial discs. *Chick*—Covered with grayish-white or buffy-white down on the upperparts but white on the undersides. Later a loose, cinnamon-buffy second down appears.

Flight Style: Close to the ground with gliding and some flapping. Hovers occasionally.

Voice: Generally silent during migration and in winter, but vocal during the breeding season. A barking *wak wak wak* repeated about 8 times; a prolonged *w-a-a-a-k*, and varied other sounds.

Nest: A shallow depression on the ground lined with weeds, grass, and some feathers. Rarely in low bushes, a depression in sand, or in an excavated burrow.

Eggs: 5 to 7 (rarely 4 to 9) white or pale creamy-white without a gloss. Incubation period is about 21 days.

Food: Rodents (especially *Microtus* voles), shrews, other small and medium-size mammals, birds occasionally, and varied insects.

Habitat: Marshes, sand dunes, fields, and plains; avoids forested or wooded areas.

North American Distribution: All of North America except the most extreme high Arctic latitudes.

BOREAL OWL *Aegolius funereus*   Plate 22

Length: 8.3 to 12.2 inches (21 to 30.9 centimeters).

Wingspread: 19.7 to 25.8 inches (50 to 65.5 centimeters).

Field Recognition: A small, tame, northern owl without ear tufts which might be confused with the Saw-whet Owl but with a *yellow bill* (black in Saw-whet Owl) and black borders to the facial discs. The subspecies *A. f. richardsoni* occurs in North America. *Adults (sexes similar)*—Deep brown on the upperparts with notable small white spots on the crown, forehead, and back of the head (streaks on the Saw-whet Owl). The white facial discs and eyebrows are bordered with black, and another black line extends downward from the eyebrows around the facial discs near the bill. The throat is white and the undersides white streaked with buffy-brown. The tail has white spots arranged in 4 or 5 rows. The eyes are yellow to yellowish-orange with black pupils; bill yellow; talons black. *Juvenal*—Unlike the adults. Dark brown on the uppersides with white eyebrows and a partly white lower facial disc. The undersides are paler brown with a whitish area in the middle of the breast. *Chick*—Covered with white down.

Flight Style: Direct with rapid wingbeats.

Voice: A high-pitched, slow, tolling, bell-like *ting ting ting ting*; also suggests the dropping of water.

Nest: Abandoned flicker or other woodpecker holes, or natural cavities in trees, generally from 10 to 25 feet above the ground.

Eggs: 4 to 6 (rarely 3 to 7), white with almost no gloss. Incubation period is 25 to 27 days.

Food: Small rodents (often *Microtus* voles), a few birds, and some insects.

Habitat: Conifer, or mixed conifer-deciduous, forests.

North American Distribution: The southern two-thirds of Alaska and Canada and (during some winters) the extreme northern portion of the contiguous United States.

NORTHERN SAW-WHET OWL
Aegolius acadicus   Plates 23, 24

Length: 7.1 to 8.6 inches (18 to 21.8 centimeters).

Wingspread: 18.1 to 22.2 inches (45.9 to 56.3 centimeters).

Field Recognition: A very small, unusually tame owl lacking ear tufts. More common than generally recognized. *Adults (sexes similar)*—Individuals of the subspecies *A. a. acadicus*, of southern Canada and the contiguous United States except the Southeast and extreme southern California and southwestern Arizona, are brown on the upperparts with small white streaks on the crown and forehead, white eyebrows, lores, and chin, white facial discs marked with buff and dark outer rims, and white spots on the hindneck and outer wing coverts. The underside is white with brown streaks, white (sometimes spotted with brown) undertail coverts, and legs buffy to buffy-white on the toes. The brown tail has 2 or 3 narrow, white bands and a white tip. Eyes yellow with black pupils; bill and talons grayish-black. The subspecies *A. a. brooksi*, of the Queen Charlotte Islands, British Columbia, is strikingly darker than the mainland race with most white areas on mainland birds being rich buffy-brown on *brooksi. Juvenal*—Dark chocolate brown, paler on the underside, with conspicuous white eyebrows and forehead. This plumage, strikingly different from the adult dress, is retained only for several weeks after fledging. *Chick*—Covered with white down which is retained for 10 to 14 days, followed by the dark brown juvenal plumage.

Flight Style: A rapid, woodpecker-like, labored, undulating flight unlike the flight style of other owls.

Voice: An anvil-like *tang-tang-tang-ing,* a three-part *skreigh-aw skreigh-aw skreigh-aw, hew-hew-hew-hew* whistles, and other notes including the famous "saw-filing" notes for which the owl is named.

Nest: Deserted flicker or other woodpecker holes, or rarely nest boxes.

Eggs: 5 or 6 (rarely 4 to 7) white, smooth, without a gloss. The incubation period is estimated between 21 and 28 days, with 26 days probably being reasonably accurate.

Food: Small rodents, shrews, bats, some small birds, and various insects.

Habitat: Coniferous or deciduous woodland and forests, woodlots, pine plantations, honeysuckle thickets, marshes, and swamps.

North American Distribution: Southern Canada southward through the contiguous United States except the southern states.

TYPES AND METHODS OF OWL WATCHING

Watching or listening to owls in their natural habitats can be separated into four types of activities: diurnal owl watching, nocturnal owl watching, watching roosting owls, and watching nesting owls. Diurnal owl watching and looking at these birds at roost sites are the most common types of owl watching among most bird watchers. In the future, however, as more people discover the pleasure you can derive from nocturnal owl watching and/or listening, it is possible that this type of effort could become extremely popular. Watching nesting owls is not recommended for recreational purposes because of the disturbance to the birds.

Diurnal Owl Watching

Owl watching during daylight hours essentially is restricted to occasional views of Short-eared Owls flying over fields or wetlands searching for food, or looking at Burrowing Owls standing outside their nest burrows. Perhaps views of Snowy Owls perched on coastal beaches, in fields, or on buildings or other elevated structures also can be enjoyed during those years (roughly every four to six) when they engage in substantial southward movements from the Arctic regions of Alaska and Canada. These birds are then observed easily, often at close range, during the day. Even more exciting are opportunities to see, during daylight, rare Arctic species such as Boreal, Great Gray, and Northern Hawk Owls

Alan Wormington

Northern Hawk Owls are diurnal. During winter invasions, they are sometimes seen in the northern United States and southern Canada.

during the very rare occasions (such as the winter of 1978–79) when these birds engage in southward invasions.

Nocturnal Owl Watching

Watching owls at night, sometimes known as "owl prowls" to bird watchers, is one of the most unusual and enjoyable ways to see (and/or hear) owls native to a particular geographic area. The technique used is relatively simple. First obtain a battery-powered cassette tape recorder and transfer onto tape cassettes the voices of species such as Common Barn, Eastern or Western Screech, Great Horned, Northern Pygmy, Barred, and Northern Saw-whet Owls from commercially available recordings. At least two minutes of recorded vocalizations should be taped for each species (repeat voices several times, if necessary, to obtain the two minutes for each species). Then secure a good, bright flashlight equipped with fully charged batteries.

Equipped with these tools, drive into the countryside on a dry and nearly windless night, between 8 p.m. and 4 a.m., and stop beside woodlots, creeks, wetlands, forests, fields, and abandoned farm buildings *away from occupied homes*. Pull off the road into a safe parking spot, stop the engine of your vehicle, get outside, and play the recordings of the various species of owls. Start with the voices of small owls such as Northern Saw-whet or Eastern or Western Screech Owls then gradually switch to the sounds of larger and more

Short-eared Owls at a winter roost in New York State.

Western Owl Silhouettes

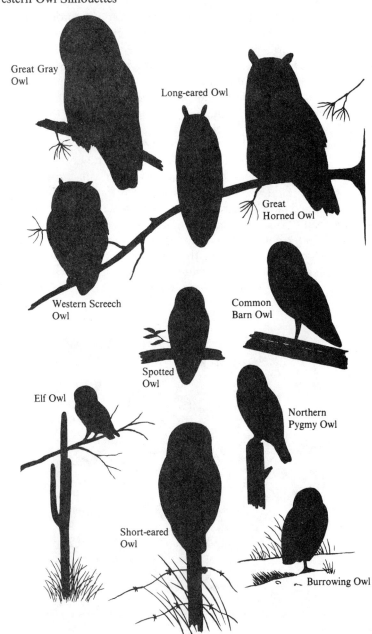

Great Gray Owl

Long-eared Owl

Great Horned Owl

Western Screech Owl

Common Barn Owl

Spotted Owl

Elf Owl

Northern Pygmy Owl

Short-eared Owl

Burrowing Owl

Eastern Owl Silhouettes

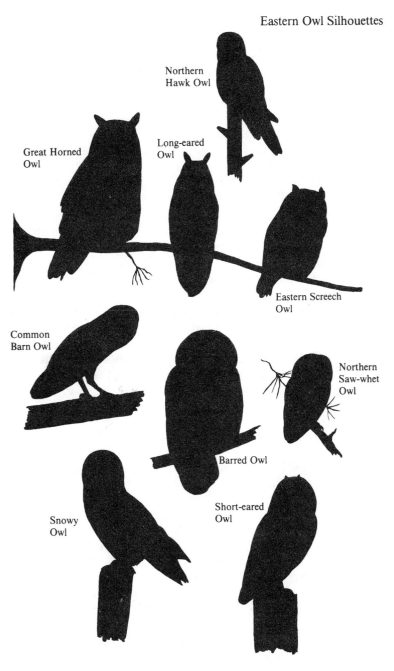

Northern
Hawk Owl

Great Horned
Owl

Long-eared
Owl

Eastern Screech
Owl

Common
Barn Owl

Northern
Saw-whet
Owl

Barred Owl

Snowy
Owl

Short-eared
Owl

Silhouette Plates by Rod Arbogast

powerful species ending with Great Horned Owl. Slowly turn the volume of the tape recorder to high (loud) in order to be certain that any owls in the area will hear the recordings. Talk to your companions very softly. Do not slam doors of vehicles. If owls are present, you should hear them within a few minutes—often almost immediately—as they respond vocally to the recordings. Not infrequently, on bright moonlit nights, Eastern Screech Owls will not only respond vocally but will fly to limbs of trees or other perches near the tape recorder. If you remain quiet, and relatively motionless, you sometimes can direct a beam of light from a flashlight onto the birds and study them in detail for several minutes before they fly away.

It is helpful to learn to recognize the outline or silhouettes of common owl species because they are usually seen first as dim shadows after they respond to the playing of tape recordings and land on a nearby branch. The owl silhouettes shown in this book will aid you in learning the shapes of the owl species commonly encountered.

Caution is necessary, however, when using tape recordings to attract owls. Never play the tapes so long, or repeatedly, in one area as to force owls from nesting territories. Owls respond to recorded sounds because they "think" another owl has invaded their territory. Thus foolish and prolonged use of this technique can cause harm to owls.

Roosting Owls

Watching roosting owls is a regularly utilized form of bird watching although some birders don't do it because they believe it disturbs the owls. To be sure, locating and watching roosting owls can disrupt the resting activities of these birds if people fail to use good judgment and needlessly create loud sounds, surround or throw sticks or other objects at the birds, or remain at active roosts for prolonged periods of time. However, brief and quiet visits to owl roosts—without attempting to cause the birds to take flight—rarely causes damage to the birds or their roost site. Indeed, watching roosting owls is an excellent way to observe and study Long-eared Owls and many other species.

Most efforts at locating roosting owls are done in stands of coniferous trees where owls tend to perch, rest, or sleep during daylight hours. To discover such birds, therefore, owl watchers visit pine woodlots and plantations and slowly walk through them while *quietly* looking for pellets on the ground beneath the trees, and whitewash (excrement) on the trunks and lower limbs of the trees or on the ground beneath them. When signs of the presence of owls are seen, a careful search of the branches of those trees sometimes reveals owls roosting among the dense vegetation. Common Barn, Long-eared, Short-eared, and Northern Saw-whet Owls tend to be particularly fond of roosting in such places.

Old buildings, church towers without screenings over openings, water towers, silos, steel support beams under bridges, and similar structures also are used commonly as roost sites by Common Barn Owls. They also are worthwhile places to check for the presence of these birds. Similarly, low honeysuckle thickets, sometimes adjacent to roads, are attractive roost sites for some Northern Saw-whet Owls and should be checked carefully for these birds. Flocks of American Crows mobbing Great Horned Owls on a roost tree also serve to alert owl watchers to the presence of these large and powerful birds. Finally, Eastern and Western Screech Owls often roost in natural holes or cavities in trees, as well as on limbs of trees outside such openings, but can be extremely difficult to see—especially when the birds are in the gray color phase and closely resemble the color of tree bark. Nevertheless, a careful binocular check of such holes can be worthwhile.

Nesting Owls

Most owls nest in late winter and early spring in a considerable variety of habitats and locations. It is possible to watch owls at their nest sites, but there is little justification for doing so for recreational owl watching purposes. Therefore, unless you are engaged in ornithological research that requires disturbance of nesting owls, *bird watchers should not visit or disturb nesting owls.* Protection and conservation of these birds must be placed before the desire to see or photograph adults at nests or nestlings.

Reading Sign

The ability to look for, and recognize, evidence of the presence of owls helps when recreational owl watching.

For example, the excrement (called whitewash) voided by owls below perches sometimes is somewhat solid, chalky, and forms little heaps on branches of deciduous trees whereas hawk whitewash often splashes and spatters on the branches. Sometimes, however, owl whitewash also can splash and spatter on conifer branches used as roost sites.

At other times, when you find feathers of a partly eaten bird, it may be possible to determine if an owl or other raptor flushed from the still-warm prey. To do this, examine the bases of the features carefully. If they are clean and smooth (as opposed to having tiny bits of flesh clinging to them) the prey was plucked while still warm indicating recent death.

The presence of owl pellets below roosts in conifer trees or elsewhere is, however, solid evidence of the presence—past or present—of owls. If the pellets are weathered, very faded gray in color, and held together loosely they probably are old. However, if they are gray and well formed, perhaps even shiny and moist, they often are very fresh and suggest the nearby presence of owls. Then a careful search of trees or branches might produce views of the birds quietly watching *your* activities.

The ability to recognize and read sign can extend one's owl watching activities considerably and add to the enjoyment and knowledge one derives from this type of nature study.

Police Relations

Sooner or later, during the course of nocturnal owl watching, local police might become curious about such seemingly strange and suspicious activities. It is wise, therefore, to have available proof that you are a bird watcher. As long as you are not causing disturbances at nearby homes in the middle of the night, there is nothing illegal about nocturnal owl watching. However, if an officer insists that you move the best course of action is to follow his directions—then follow up the incident with a polite letter to the local chief of police the next day in which you explain your activities (and perhaps invite him to go along owl watching on your next trip).

OWL WATCHING EQUIPMENT

A variety of equipment is helpful in owl watching. The items discussed here are particularly useful and should be included in every recreational owl watcher's field pack or home study area.

Binoculars

Because most species of owls are nocturnal, binoculars are less important to owl watchers than to hawk watchers, although they are very helpful when looking at diurnal owls and occasionally even when watching the nocturnal species. Good quality 7×35, 7×50, or 8×40 birding binoculars are satisfactory for owl watching with those providing the most light-gathering capability and brightest images being the most useful.

Telescope

A birding telescope, equipped with a 20× (or higher) eyepiece, also is helpful for close views of some diurnal owls. The telescope can be mounted on a photographic tripod for support, or fastened onto a gunstock or other shoulder support.

Tape Recorder

A small, portable, battery powered, cassette tape recorder is extremely helpful when trying to locate owls at night. By playing the recorded voices of Common Barn, Eastern or Western Screech, Great Horned, Barred, Northern Pygmy, and Northern Saw-whet Owls—and perhaps other species—in suitable owl habitats some species will respond vocally and reveal their presence. Eastern Screech Owls, for example, often approach the spot where the tape recorder is placed thus allowing owl watchers to observe them at relatively close range. Full details are not yet available on which species of owls respond to recordings of their voices, so owl watchers will want to experiment with recordings of various species. Again: *Never play owl voice recordings so long or repeatedly during the breeding season as to cause a breeding pair of birds to abandon their nesting efforts.* The safety of the birds always must be placed before observation of the owls.

Records

Several commercial records of bird songs contain the voices of various species of owls, and it is from these that you may transfer for private use the sounds of selected species onto tape cassettes for use in the field during night owl prowls. Among the recordings recommended especially are *A Field Guide to Bird Songs* and *A Field Guide to Western Bird Songs* produced in the Peterson field guide series under the direction of the Cornell University Laboratory of Ornithology and published by Houghton Mifflin Company.

Flashlight

A strong flashlight is very useful and helpful to owl watchers looking for these birds at night, especially if used in combination with a tape recorder. For best results, wait until the birds respond to the owl recordings and begin to approach the source of the sound (the recorder). Try to spot the owls by moonlight or look for an owl's silhouette as it lands on a nearby branch, then shine the beam of the flashlight onto the bird for better viewing opportunities. Remember, however, that it is not legal to spotlight wildlife in some states so be certain of the laws. A telephone call to a local wildlife conservation officer or district game warden, or to a state's wildlife agency, should be adequate to determine the status of spotlighting laws or regulations.

Pellet Bag

When looking for owls at roost sites, it is useful to carry an inexpensive plastic bag into which pellets can be placed. Also add a small amount of paradichlorobenzene (PDB) or a few mothballs to kill any insects or larvae present in the pellets. Then, after you return home, the pellets can be examined, picked apart, and the prey items identified.

Mammal Identification Guides

Rodents and other small mammals form a large proportion of the diets of many species of owls. It is helpful, therefore, to learn how to recognize various mammalian prey species from the skulls contained in owl pellets. Indeed, pellet content analysis is so useful to professional wildlife biologists that it is one of the standard methods of determining the diets of owls. To become a good owl watcher, therefore, one should also become something of a mammalogist. Several good books are available in which keys to mammal skull identification are provided. Among them are those listed below.

BOOTH, ERNEST S. 1961. *How to Know the Mammals.* Second Edition. William C. Brown Co., Publishers, Dubuque, Iowa.

BURT, WILLIAM H. 1957. *Mammals of the Great Lakes Region.* University of Michigan Press, Ann Arbor, Michigan.

BURT, WILLIAM H. and RICHARD P. GROSSENHEIDER. 1952. *A Field Guide to the Mammals.* Houghton Mifflin Co., Boston, Massachusetts.

HALL, E. RAYMOND and KEITH R. KELSON. 1959. *The Mammals of North America.* Ronald Press Co., New York, N.Y.

HOFFMEISTER, DONALD F. and CARL O. MOHR. 1957. *Fieldbook of Illinois Mammals. Manual 4.* Illinois Natural History Survey, Urbana, Illinois.

Synoptic Skull Collection

Not infrequently the skulls of rodents, shrews, and other mammals are recovered intact or nearly so from owl pellets. Thus one may easily identify the prey consumed by owls merely by identifying the small mammal skulls removed from pellets.

A representative or synoptic collection of correctly identified rodent, shrew, bat, and other small mammal skulls is of great value and help to persons wishing to learn to recognize the anatomical characteristics of various prey species. Most natural history museums, and many state museums with natural history departments, have collections of native mammals. In most instances these collections contain cleaned skulls. Many museum curators will gladly cooperate or assist in helping interested persons identify skulls they recover from pellets. They also may provide suggestions for the development of your own synoptic mammal skull collection. Not infrequently the best skulls (those intact or with the least damage) removed from pellets can be saved for this purpose. Occasionally some museums discard specimens from their collections and it may be possible to secure such materials provided state or federal permits are not required to retain such specimens. Your local wildlife conservation officer, or state wildlife agency, can determine for you which species may be kept legally without permits.

In order to keep a synoptic skull collection free of insect pests, put the specimens into an airtight container into which is also placed a small amount of paradichlorobenzene (PDB) or ordinary mothballs. These chemicals should be replaced every few months, but they also should keep the collection free of insects. It is important, however, to avoid breathing vapors from the chemicals for prolonged periods of time. Nevertheless, their use is standard museum technique to protect zoological collections.

OWL PELLETS AND FOOD HABITS

Aside from observing owls in their natural habitats, collecting and studying owl pellets is one of the most enjoyable and educational aspects of owl watching. Indeed, few activities available to bird watchers and other interested persons allow better opportunities to see the results of predator-prey interactions in wildlife communities and gain vivid insights into the food habits of owls.

Pellets

Pellets are masses of bones, fur, skulls, feathers, and other materials that owls are unable to digest. They are ejected through the mouth, often at nest or roost sites, and thus are relatively easy to find as they accumulate (sometimes in large quantities) on the ground beneath these sites. It is easy, therefore, to gather a collection of pellets, place them in a plastic bag, and carry them home for later content examination.

When owl watchers explore pine plantations, and other likely sites used by owls, pellets frequently remain and are discovered after the birds no longer use a site. Therefore, the following general guide to owl pellet characteristics will help interested persons to identify pellets from various species. To further aid in identification, it is equally helpful to develop a collection of owl pellets of known identity such as those gathered at active owl roosts. Unidentified pellets then can be compared directly with the correctly identified reference pellets. After a little field and study experience, you should become skilled at making reasonably accurate pellet identifications by simple inspection of the pellets.

To study the contents of owl pellets, as I pointed out in *A Manual for Bird Watching in the Americas,* place the pellets on an old newspaper and allow them to dry in the air. Then

Owl Pellet Guide

Species	*Size*	*Characteristics*
Common Barn Owl	Fairly large	Cylindrical, containing several prey remains.
Screech Owls (Eastern and Western)	Medium	Oval, compact, dark gray when ejected.
Whiskered Screech Owl	Small	Loosely formed; disintegrate rapidly.
Flammulated Owl	Small	Loosely formed, contain insect parts.
Great Horned Owl	Very large	Dark grayish-black, compact, with numerous bones, teeth, skull parts, fur, feathers, and claws. Color changes to slate-gray several days after being ejected.
Snowy Owl	Large	Cylindrical, compact, with numerous bones, parts of skulls, feathers, and fur.
Northern Hawk Owl	Small	Gray, mucus-coated.
Northern Pygmy Owl	Very small	Pellets rarely formed; those that are disintegrate upon ejection or very shortly thereafter.
Ferruginous Pygmy Owl	Small	Elongated-oval, very compact.
Elf Owl	Tiny	Dry, loose, poorly formed, disintegrate soon after ejection.
Burrowing Owl	Small	Smooth, brown.
Barred Owl	Large	Compact.
Spotted Owl	Large	Compact.
Great Gray Owl	Very large	Contains various bones, skulls, fur, and feathers.
Long-eared Owl	Fairly large	Oval to cylindrical, gray, compact.
Short-eared Owl	Fairly large	Oval to cylindrical, dark gray, mucus-covered.
Boreal Owl	Small	Dark gray.
Northern Saw-whet Owl	Small	Dark gray, compact.

use forceps to pick them apart, separating skulls and other bones from fur and other matter. Many mammal skulls found in owl pellets are intact (or nearly so) because owls swallow large chunks of food when they eat. This makes identification of small mammal skulls relatively easy—especially after you gain some experience sorting and identifying prey remains.

Use of identification keys to mammal skulls, contained in one of the reference books recommended earlier, is essential at least until you gain knowledge of skull features. Pellet study will teach you about the lives of owls in addition to the food being taken—types of habitats in which the birds were active, and the relative population abundance and vulnerability of various prey species. Sometimes an unexpected find is made—some rare or unusual mammal seldom reported from a particular geographic area. Indeed, small mammals entirely unknown from an area occasionally appear in owl pellets thus resulting in mammal species being listed as new to an area.

To derive the most information from studying the contents of owl pellets, gather certain related information in the field when the pellets are collected. Date, location, habitat type, and identification of owls seen at a roost or nest all should be noted on a small piece of paper for each site then placed in the pellet bag with the pellets from the site in question. Later this information will allow you to compare seasonal, location, and species food habit differences thus giving you a much better understanding of the role of owl predation in the wildlife communities where the birds live.

Food Habits

Learning about the food habits of various species of owls is the primary purpose of collecting and examining the contents of owl pellets. It has been used for decades by wildlife biologists to arrive at approximations of the general statements of dietary habits of owls. Such general food habit statements are included earlier in this book in the species accounts. However, it is clear to anybody who has ever studied owl pellets for long periods of time, from many geographic areas, that certain prey species are especially important dietary items to owls. *Microtus* voles, for example, are especially important to many owls (and numerous other predators)—especially Common Barn Owls, but many other species as well. Deer mice of the genus *Peromyscus* also frequently appear in pellets of many owls. Various species of other rats and mice also sometimes form significant percentages in owl diets. Persons wishing to receive a general non-technical introduction to owl (and hawk) food habit ecology may find my *Hawks and Owls of North America* a good starting point whereas John and Frank Craighead's *Hawks, Owls and Wildlife* provides a more technical and detailed presentation of owl and other raptor food habit ecology.

OWL MIGRATIONS AND INVASIONS

The geographic movements of owls are known much less perfectly than those of diurnal birds of prey such as hawks, eagles, and falcons. Nevertheless some owl species engage in seasonal migrations, or at least wander southward for short distances during severe winters, whereas others occasionally exhibit marked (and spectacular) southward invasions. Despite these movements, most owls in North America are relatively sedentary birds—permanent residents in the areas in which they live. It is some of the migratory species, however, that exhibit great appeal to owl watchers because some are Arctic or boreal birds and observed very infrequently (if not rarely) by most bird watchers. Many of these owls also are diurnal and extremely tame. Thus the ease with which they can be seen makes them even more appealing. Not only can they be approached much more closely than more familiar owl species, they also offer owl watchers superb opportunities to study the birds at close range and at leisure. Exceptional opportunities are available, therefore, to study and record visual behavior displays of the types discussed by Donald W. Stokes in *A Guide to the Behavior of Common Birds.* For most owls, such visual displays are poorly known or unknown. Similarly, photographers have remarkable opportunities to photograph these birds.

Seasonal Migrations

In exceptionally severe winters many species of owls may move slightly southward for short periods of time, but normally Common Barn, Snowy, Long-eared, Flammulated, Elf, and Northern Saw-whet Owls are the migratory species. Common Barn Owls, for example, exhibit a clear migratory pattern in respect to those individuals (especially juvenile birds) that live north of 35 degrees North latitude. Similarly Long-eared Owls, especially western birds, migrate southward from December to March. Elf Owls also migrate southward from the United States during the winter, and the delightful Northern Saw-whet Owl now is known to follow specific migration routes. In autumn, for example, Northern Saw-whets move from central Ontario southwestward into Kentucky, southward along the Atlantic coastline from Maine to North Carolina, and southward along the western shore of Lake Michigan. Similar routes also are used in spring.

Invasions

In addition to the seasonal migrations of certain species of owls, some of the boreal and Arctic owls engage in true invasions from time to time. When such extensive movements occur, very large numbers of the birds fly southward and appear well into the contiguous United States. Owl watchers wishing to learn more about wildlife cycles and related phenomena should read David Lack's *The Natural Regulation of Animal Numbers* and Lloyd B. Keith's *Wildlife's Ten-Year Cycle.*

The best known, and most frequent in occurrence, of these invasions is that exhibited by the Snowy Owl. Since 1882, Snowy Owl invasions occurred roughly every three, four, or five years. Apparently the southward movements are correlated with the population crash of prey species, especially lemmings, upon which the splendid white owls feed.

Occasionally other far northern owls also engage in southward invasions. Thus the splendid Northern Hawk Owl sometimes appears in the northern border states during severe winters, and during major invasions may penetrate much farther south. Even more exciting are the extremely rare invasions of the Great Gray Owl—an absolutely mag-

Three Great Gray Owls on Amherst Island, Ontario, Canada, during the 1978–79 owl invasion.

nificent bird. More than 334 Great Gray Owls engaged in a massive southward invasion into northeastern North America during the winter of 1978–79. Not since the winter of 1890–91, almost a century earlier, have so many of these spectacular birds appeared in the area. While most individuals were seen in New England and northern and central New York State, some birds ventured south as far as Long Island.

Amherst Island, Ontario, three miles southwest of Kingston, produced the largest and most remarkable density of owls during the 1978–79 invasion. The estimated owl population on the island during the period January to mid-April 1979 was 160 birds of 10 species. Apparently the island supported a very large population of prey animals, chiefly small rodents, upon which the various owls preyed.

As one might expect, bird watchers from all over North America visited Amherst Island during the winter of 1978–79 to observe and photograph the splendid assortment of owls reported there. Such large concentrations of owls, of course, are only temporary situations and are subject to many complex ecological factors.

SURVIVAL ADAPTATIONS

Because most owl species are nocturnal animals they have evolved a variety of remarkable adaptations which enable them to survive as creatures of the night. Some of these survival adaptations are discussed here.

Vision

There is an old myth that owls are blind, or can't see during the day. Both ideas, of course, are wrong. Indeed, owls have excellent eyesight—so excellent, in fact, that many species are fully capable of seeing well even when light is so dim as to be almost gone. On the other hand, when very bright light conditions occur owls merely close the iris of each eye to pinpoint size to compensate for the brightness. Owls even are capable of changing the iris opening of each eye independently of each other.

Because owls have so many rod cells packed together into their eyes, in order to achieve maximum visual ability even under the poorest light conditions, they have lost many cone cells which are present in the eyes of many other animals and allow color vision. Thus owls apparently see only in shades of gray rather than the color spectrum we see. In short, owls are color blind.

In addition, the eyes of owls are fixed in their sockets in the skull. They can't be moved as the human eye can. Therefore, owls must turn their heads in whatever direction they wish to see and are fully able of rotating their heads about 270 degrees. To see beyond that point, they almost instantly snap their heads around in the other direction. Owls also have binocular vision to achieve three dimension vision, and even augment that survival adaptation by sometimes using various head sways and bobs to increase their triangulation capability.

Hearing

Because most owls are nocturnal animals one would assume that they have a well developed sense of hearing. Research confirms the assumption. In the Common Barn Owl, for example, biologist Roger Payne demonstrated experimentally that the birds are able to use the sounds of prey on the ground—such as rodents running—to triangulate to the source of the sound and capture the prey. Acute hearing, therefore, is fully as important a survival adaptation as is keen vision. The Common Barn Owl's large but differently shaped ear openings, placed on each side of the head at different locations, permitted use of sound triangulation to locate and capture prey.

Feathers

Owl feathers also are especially adapted to enhance survival of these birds. The flight feathers in particular have frayed edges so the birds make a minimum of noise when flying. This special softness on the edges of the flight feathers is especially notable on nocturnal species such as Great Horned or Eastern and Western Screech Owls; it is less notable on the diurnal owl species.

Some owl species—Great Horned, Eastern and Western Screech, and Long-eared are examples—also have more or less well developed ear tufts which have no relationship to hearing. Instead, they are feather tufts located on the top of the head and are not normally elevated. However, when danger is present, the ear tufts are then erected and serve either to make the birds appear larger and more dangerous than they are, or allow the owls to blend into the surrounding background or environment to avoid detection.

Bills and Talons

Like most birds of prey, owls also have strong bills and talons which enable them to capture and eat prey of various sizes. The sharp talons, of course, are connected to powerful muscles and tendons thus allowing the owls to grasp and kill prey quickly. Then the powerful bills are used to pull large chunks of the prey apart, although owls sometimes swallow all or most of their prey whole. That is one reason why biologists and owl watchers often find entire prey skulls intact in owl pellets.

Size and Color

In hawks, eagles, and falcons, there is striking sexual dimorphism in that females are about a third larger than males of the same species. In owls this sexual dimorphism is somewhat less obvious but nevertheless is present.

At the same time, there may or may not be differences in coloration between the sexes of a particular owl species. In the case of Eastern Screech Owls, red and gray color phases occur regardless of age or sex. Indeed, some broods of nestling Eastern Screech Owls contain birds of both color phases. On the other hand, female Snowy Owls are marked more boldly than males. In some species, such as Northern Saw-whet Owls, nestlings also wear a juvenal plumage strikingly different in color and pattern from the adult plumage. Finally, various subspecies of owls often exhibit variations in coloration as well. In the case of the Great Horned Owl, this can vary from very dark to nearly white depending upon where the birds live.

OWL CONSERVATION

Owls are fascinating, and there are many ways owl watchers and birders can aid the conservation and survival of these predatory birds. Each of the following projects can help to improve the nesting success of specific species or the overall welfare of owls. I urged all people interested in owls to become active owl conservationists.

Owl Nest Structures

Some species, such as Common Barn Owls and Eastern and Western Screech Owls, readily accept nest boxes. Others, such as Great Horned Owls, sometimes accept nest boxes or other artificial structures on which to nest. Construction and placement of the structures provide excellent owl conservation opportunities for these species. Some of the structures are based on the work and experiments of raptor biologist Frances Hamerstrom in Wisconsin, others (such as Common Barn Owl boxes) follow suggestions from Professor Carl D. Marti in Utah, and still others are based upon some of my own experiences working with owls.

Owl watchers should understand, however, that the nest box sizes presented here should be considered only as general guidelines. Conservationists should conduct their own experiments with sizes and shapes of nest boxes to try to develop better or more effective structures. The results can be very rewarding.

Owl Nest Box Dimensions (Sizes in Inches)

Species	Floor of Box	Height of Box	Entrance above Floor	Size of Entrance
Common Barn Owl	24×24	19	11	8×10
Eastern Screech Owl	8×8	12–15	8–10	3×3
Western Screech Owl	8×8	12–15	8–10	3×3
Great Horned Owl	18×20	24–26	5–18	14×14
Barred Owl	13×15	21–24	15–17	8×8
Great Gray Owl	18×20	24–26	5–18	14×14
Boreal Owl	6×6	10-12	8–10	2¾×2¾
Northern Saw-whet Owl	6×6	10–12	8–10	2¾×2¾

Source: *Birds of Prey of Wisconsin* by Frances Hamerstrom (Wisconsin Department of Natural Resources, 1972). Common Barn Owl data provided by Professor Carl D. Marti.

Common Barn Owl

The Common Barn Owl, distributed widely throughout most of the contiguous United States, readily accepts nest boxes in which to raise its young. There is no fixed size required for the construction of these boxes, but generally a plywood box with the sizes indicated in the table is adequate. As in all nest boxes, drain holes in the floor of the box should be provided.

Place these nest boxes in or near the tops of silos, in dark corners high in barns, in church towers, or in other buildings or structures where cats or other mammal predators are less likely to prowl. The structures also can be put in tall trees, but other creatures may beat the owls to the boxes.

Don't forget to put some sawdust or hay on the bottom of the box to prevent the owl's eggs from rolling during incubation.

Screech Owls

Both the Eastern and Western Screech Owls readily accept nest boxes. Since these birds occur in a variety of habitats across North America, you can try using the boxes almost anywhere the birds are found, but generally orchards, suburbs, edges of woodland along running waterways, and similar locations tend to be the most productive. Since

American Kestrels also use nest boxes of approximately the size used by these owls, don't be surprised to find these small falcons using some of your boxes.

Great Horned Owl

These powerful owls generally nest on abandoned crow or hawk platforms, but occasionally they will also nest in natural tree cavities. Putting old rubber tires high in tree forks in farmland, woodlots, or forested areas can help to provide horned owls with artificial nest platforms.

Alternatively, use of special owl boxes placed in similar habitats may attract some Great Horned Owls. Approximate box sizes are provided in the table. As in other boxes, don't forget to put some drainage holes in the floor and a little hay or sawdust in the bottom of the box upon which the female may deposit her eggs.

Barred Owl

Barred Owls also occasionally use nest boxes as breeding sites if the structures are provided in habitats such as wooded areas near streams, in swamps, or similar locations. Experiment with boxes if the birds are known to occur in an area. Your efforts could enhance the population density of the species.

Great Gray Owl

The Great Gray Owl is a magnificent species which nests mostly in Canada, Alaska, and some locations in the northern contiguous states. Considerable experimentation is needed in the use of nest boxes for these birds, but it is worthwhile to put some boxes in boreal woodland and bogs in the hope that some Great Gray Owls may accept them as nest sites.

Boreal Owl

Nest boxes of the appropriate size, placed in woodland and swamps in the northern breeding range of this species, will provide suitable nesting sites for these small owls.

Northern Saw-whet Owl

These are among the most delightful of all North American owls and the birds do accept nest boxes as nest sites. Put the boxes, either the size used for Eastern or Western Screech Owls or slightly smaller (see table), in woodland, swamps, and along the edges of marshes and other wetlands.

Additional Conservation Measures

In addition to taking direct action to aid owls, such as building and putting nest boxes in suitable locations, owl watchers and birders can further the cause of owl conservation by urging farmers to protect owls living on their property, by pointing out to sportsmen that owls are important and desirable parts of wildlife communities and that these birds are protected by law and must not be shot, and by generally promoting owl and other raptor conservation in meetings, discussions, and during similar situations. Owl watchers also should make efforts to inform local police departments that owls are protected and should not be shot when police receive complaints about Eastern Screech Owls or other species defending nest territories or nestlings. Close cooperation between police departments and state and federal wildlife law enforcement agents should be encouraged.

Finally, as I stressed earlier in this book, I do not recommend that recreational owl watchers disturb or visit owl nest sites during the breeding season. There is no important reason why owl watchers, bird watchers, or bird listeners should inflict unnecessary disturbance or stress upon nesting owls. Leave nesting owls alone. It is a critical time in their annual cycle.

IDENTIFICATION PLATES AND FIELD MARKS

Plate 1   **Common Barn Owl**   pp. 1–3

Adult (white phase)
1. Facial disk heart-shaped or rounded.
2. Eyes dark.
3. Upperparts tawny or golden-brown.
4. Underparts white, sometimes with brown flecks.
5. Legs long.

Adult (orange phase)
1. Similar to white phase.
2. Upperparts tawny or golden-brown.
3. Underparts tawny or golden-brown.

Immature
1. Similar to adult but with more down visible.
2. Facial disk heart-shaped or rounded.

Flight Style
1. Swift, graceful, light.
2. Shifts from side to side.

Plate 1   COMMON BARN OWL   57

Common Barn Owl—adult at nest with eggs.

Common Barn Owl—adult at nest with nestlings.

Plate 2 **Eastern Screech Owl** pp. 3–5

Adult (gray phase)
1. Upperparts gray or grayish-brown with streaks.
2. Underparts white with dark streaks.
3. Ear tufts small.
4. Small size.
5. Irises yellow.

Flight Style
1. Rapid, steady wingbeats.
2. Occasionally brief glides.
3. Hovers rarely.

Plate 2 EASTERN SCREECH OWL   59

Eastern Screech Owl—adult (gray phase).

Alan Wormington

Plate 3   **Eastern Screech Owl**   pp. 3–5

Adult (red phase)
1. Upperparts reddish to cinnamon-rufous.
2. Underparts whitish with reddish or rufous bars and streaks.
3. Ear tufts small.
4. Small size.
5. Irises yellow.

Flight Style
1. Rapid, steady wingbeats.
2. Occasionally brief glides.
3. Hovers rarely.

Plate 3   EASTERN SCREECH OWL   61

Donald S. Heintzelman

Eastern Screech Owl—adult (red phase).

Plate 4   **Eastern Screech Owl**   pp. 3–5

Adult (gray phase)
1. Upperparts gray or grayish-brown with streaks.
2. Underparts white with dark streaks.
3. Ear tufts small.
4. Small size.
5. Irises yellow.

Adult (red phase)
1. Upperparts reddish to cinnamon-rufous.
2. Underparts whitish with reddish or rufous bars and streaks.
3. Ear tufts small.
4. Small size.
5. Irises yellow.

Flight Style
1. Rapid, steady wingbeats.
2. Occasionally brief glides.
3. Hovers rarely.

Plate 4   EASTERN SCREECH OWL   **63**

Eastern Screech Owl—roosting.

Eastern Screech Owl—adult (gray phase).

Eastern Screech Owl—flying.

Plate 5   **Western Screech Owl**   pp. 5–6

Adult
1. Voice and range separate from Eastern Screech Owl.
2. Upperparts gray with darker streaks.
3. Underparts somewhat lighter with fine bars (bolder in Whiskered Screech Owl).
4. Ear tufts small.
5. Small size.
6. Irises yellow.
7. Red color phase rare (coastal Alaska to coastal Oregon).

Juvenal
1. Less well marked than adult.
2. Other field marks similar to adult.

Flight Style
1. Rapid, steady wingbeats.
2. Occasionally brief glides.
3. Hovers rarely.

Plate 5   WESTERN SCREECH OWL   65

Western Screech Owl—adult roosting.

Western Screech Owl—nestlings.

Plate 6   **Whiskered Screech Owl**   pp. 7–8

Adult (sexes similar)
1. Smaller, but similar to, Western Screech Owl.
2. Underside more boldly barred than Western Screech Owl.
3. Ear tufts small.
4. Irises yellow.
5. Voice, habitat, and range different from Western Screech Owl and Flammulated Owl.

Flammulated Owl   pp. 8–9

Adult
1. Eyes dark (not yellow).
2. Size small.
3. Ear tufts small.
4. Facial disks with rufous edge.
5. Back with two rufous shoulder stripes.

Plate 6 WHISKERED SCREECH OWL/FLAMMULATED OWL **67**

Don Bleitz

Whiskered Screech Owl—perched.

Don Bleitz

Flammulated Owl—female.

Plate 7   **Great Horned Owl**   pp. 9–11

Adult
1. Very large and robust.
2. Ear tufts large, placed wide apart.
3. Head large.
4. Throat white.
5. Irises yellow.
6. Upperparts brown.
7. Underparts lighter and barred.

Flight Style
1. Heavy, among trees.
2. Sometimes soars just above ground.

Plate 7   GREAT HORNED OWL   69

Donald S. Heintzelman

Harry Goldman

Great Horned Owl—adult
(New York State).

Great Horned Owl—adult
(eastern Pennsylvania).

Ray Quigley

Great Horned Owl—adult (California).

Plate 8   **Great Horned Owl**   pp. 9–11

Nestling
1. Down covered.
2. Irises yellow, pupils blue (not black as in adult).

Juvenal
1. Wings and tail similar to adult.
2. Ear tufts shorter than adult.
3. White throat smaller and duller than adult.
4. Plumage ruddier than adult.

Plate 8   GREAT HORNED OWL   71

Harry Goldman

Great Horned Owl—nestlings (4–5 days old).

Ron Quigley

Great Horned Owl—nestlings (several weeks old).

Plate 9   **Snowy Owl**   pp. 11–12

Adult (male)
1. Pure white or nearly so.
2. Ear tufts absent.
3. Irises yellow.
4. Large.

Adult (female)
1. White with brownish spots on upperparts and under-parts.
2. Irises yellow.
3. Large.

Flight Style
1. Strong, steady, direct.
2. Body undulates.
3. Head turns back and forth.

Plate 9   SNOWY OWL   73

Snowy Owl—adult male.

Snowy Owl—adult female.

Snowy Owl—adult male.

Plate 10   **Northern Hawk Owl**   pp. 12–13

Adult
1. Hawk-like shape.
2. Medium size.
3. Facial disks bordered with black.
4. Underparts barred.
5. Tail long.
6. Diurnal habits.
7. Uses exposed hunting perches.

Flight Style
1. Falcon-like.
2. Rapid, erratic wingbeats, direct.
3. Occasionally hovers.
4. *Accipiter*-like in woodland.

Plate 10   NORTHERN HAWK OWL   75

Northern Hawk Owl—adult.   Northern Hawk Owl—adult.

Northern Hawk Owl—adult.

Plate 11   **Northern Pygmy Owl**   pp. 13–14

Adult (gray phase)
1. No ear tufts.
2. Upperparts grayish-brown spotted with white.
3. Two black nape patches.
4. Sides grayish-brown spotted with white.
5. Underparts white with black streaks.
6. Tail long with narrow white bands.

Adult (red phase)
1. Similar to gray phase but chestnut rather than grayish-brown.

Flight Style
1. Short flight with rapid wingbeats.
2. Suggests a shrike or American Kestrel.

Plate 11   NORTHERN PYGMY OWL   **77**

Northern Pygmy Owl—adult.

William C. Shuster

Plate 12   **Ferruginous Pygmy Owl**   pp. 14–15

Adult (red phase)
1. Small, rusty-backed.
2. Forehead spotted with white.
3. Undersides streaked with brown (not black).

Adult (gray phase)
1. Upperparts gray with brownish.
2. Tail slaty-gray with black bands.

Elf Owl   pp. 15–16

Adult (gray phase)
1. Tiny, no ear tufts.
2. Irises yellow.
3. Undersides buffy.

Adult (brown phase)
1. Similar to gray phase.
2. Darker brownish on back.

Plate 12   FERRUGINOUS PYGMY OWL/ELF OWL   79

Ferruginous Pygmy Owl—perched at nest hole.

Don Bleitz

Elf Owl—adult male perched.

Don Bleitz

Plate 13   **Burrowing Owl**   pp. 16–17

Adult
1. Head rounded.
2. Black throat band.
3. Undersides barred.
4. Frequently bobbs head.

Flight Style
1. Flies close to ground.
2. Wingbeats labored.
3. Hovers when hunting.

Plate 13   BURROWING OWL   81

Burrowing Owl—adult.

Burrowing Owl—adult.

Plate 14   **Spotted Owl**   pp. 17–18

Adult
1. Head rounded, no ear tufts.
2. Eyes dark.
3. Upperparts dark brown.
4. Underparts barred with horizontal whitish blotches and dots (vertical streaks on Barred Owl).

Flight Style
1. Buoyant.
2. Uses heavy wingbeats.

Plate 14   SPOTTED OWL   83

David B. Johnson

Spotted Owl—adult.

Arthur M. Panzer

Spotted Owl—adult.

Plate 15   **Barred Owl**   pp. 18–19

Adult
1. Head rounded, no ear tufts.
2. Horizontal throat barring.
3. Vertical breast streaks.
4. Partly diurnal.

Flight Style
1. Buoyant, slow, heavy wingbeats.
2. Rarely soars.
3. Flies high and silently.

Plate 15   BARRED OWL   85

Harry Goldman

Mark Nyhof

Barred Owl—adult.

Barred Owl—adult.

Allan D. Cruickshank

Barred Owl—nestling.

Plate 16   **Great Gray Owl**   pp. 19–20

Adult
1. Huge.
2. No ear tufts.
3. Facial disks large and round.
4. Irises yellow.
5. Black chin spot and white "bow tie" across throat.

Plate 16   GREAT GRAY OWL   87

Great Gray Owl—adult.

Great Gray Owl—adult.

Great Gray Owl—adult.

Great Gray Owl—adult.

Plate 17   **Great Gray Owl**   pp. 19–20

Adult
1. Huge.
2. No ear tufts.
3. Facial disks large and round.
4. Irises yellow.
5. Black chin spot and white "bow tie" across throat.

Flight Style
1. Slow, measured, for short distances.
2. Flies not far above the ground.

Plate 17   GREAT GRAY OWL   89

Great Gray Owl—adult.

Great Gray Owl—flying.

Plate 18   **Long-eared Owl**   pp. 20–21

Adult
1. Slender with ear tufts placed close together.
2. Facial disks orange-brownish.
3. Undersides streaked lengthwise.
4. Medium size.

Juvenal
1. Facial disks darker cinnamon-red than adults.
2. Ear tufts smaller.
3. Eyebrows black.

Plate 18   LONG-EARED OWL   **91**

Long-eared Owl—adult.

Long-eared Owl—adult.

Long-eared Owl—adult.

Long-eared Owl—adult.

Plate 19   **Long-eared Owl**   pp. 20–21

Flight Style
1. Buoyant and light.
2. Occasionally hovers butterfly-like.
3. Sometimes glides.

Plate 19   LONG-EARED OWL   93

Long-eared Owl—flying.

Long-eared Owl—nestling.

Plate 20   **Short-eared Owl**   pp. 21–23

Adult (male)
1. Medium size.
2. Diurnal behavior.
3. Head rounded.
4. Ear tufts tiny, barely visible even under ideal conditions.
5. Eyebrows white.
6. Irises yellow.
7. Undersides vertically streaked with brown.

Adult (female)
1. Larger than male.
2. Darker than male.

Plate 20   SHORT-EARED OWL   95

Short-eared Owl—adult.   Short-eared Owl—adult.

Short-eared Owl—adult.

Plate 21   **Short-eared Owl**   pp. 21–23

Flight Style
1. Gliding and flapping close to the ground.
2. Hovers occasionally.

Plate 21   SHORT-EARED OWL   97

Short-eared Owl—flying.

Harry Goldman

Short-eared Owl—nestlings.

Ray Quigley

Plate 22   **Boreal Owl**   pp. 23–24

Adult
1. Small, tame.
2. Forehead, crown, and back of head spotted with white (streaked in Northern Saw-whet Owl).
3. Bill yellow (black in Northern Saw-whet Owl).
4. Facial disks edged with black.
5. Scapulars spotted with white.

Juvenal
1. Small, tame.
2. Dark brown.
3. Eyebrows white.
4. Cheek spots white.

Plate 22   BOREAL OWL   99

Alan Wormington

Boreal Owl—adult.

Randy Korotev

Boreal Owl—exceptional tameness.

Randy Korotev

Boreal Owl—adult.

Plate 23   Northern Saw-whet Owl pp. 24–25

Adult

1. Small, tame.
2. Facial disks lacking black edge.
3. Forehead streaked (spotted with white in Boreal Owl).
4. Bill dark (yellow in Boreal Owl).
5. Tail short.

Plate 23   NORTHERN SAW-WHET OWL   101

Mark Nyhof

Alan Wormington

Northern Saw-whet Owl—adult.

Northern Saw-whet Owl—
regurgitating pellet.

Alan Wormington

Mark Nyhof

Northern Saw-whet Owl—adult.

Northern Saw-whet Owl—adult.

Plate 24   **Northern Saw-whet Owl pp. 24–25**

Adult
  1. Small, tame.
  2. Facial disks lacking black edge.
  3. Forehead streaked (spotted with white in Bóreal Owl).
  4. Bill dark (yellow in Boreal Owl).
  5. Tail short.

Juvenal
  1. Small, tame.
  2. Upperparts dark brown.
  3. Underparts buffy.
  4. Forehead marked with white triangle.

Plate 24   NORTHERN SAW-WHET OWL   **103**

Northern Saw-whet Owl—adult.

Northern Saw-whet Owl—juvenal.

OWL WATCHING SITES

The following sites represent only a fraction of the locations in North America where it *may* be possible to see, or hear, owls at various seasons of the year. However, bird watchers should not develop unrealistic expectations regarding what to expect to see, or hear, at these sites. Unlike hawk watching lookouts in North America, where you almost always see at least a few birds on a visit to a good lookout, owl watching sites are much less predictable. Sometimes birds will be seen or heard—but not on every visit. If a site fails to produce birds try again at a later date. Use of these sites sometimes is sporadic—for several months or years, then vacated, only to be reused again at a later date.

Bird watchers should realize, however, that considerable effort frequently is necessary to enjoy success in owl watching. Aside from those locations where Arctic species such as Snowy Owls can be seen readily in winter merely by making binocular or telescope searches from your vehicle, locating owls usually requires much more work to produce much less success. Not infrequently, for example, you must hike across many acres of pine plantations or woodlots searching every tree for owls. Or, you'll drive for miles along rural roads at night, make frequent stops to listen for or play owl voice tapes in an effort to locate elusive species, only to locate small numbers of birds. Clearly, owl watching is not the type of bird watching everybody will enjoy. It is too demanding. But, for those birders with more-than-ordinary zeal, owl watching at the following sites and countless others is educational and worthwhile.

United States

Arizona

CAVE CREEK CANYON (near Portal)

Owls Present: Whiskered Screech, Flammulated, Northern Pygmy, Elf, and Spotted.
Description: Several locations in the Cave Creek Canyon area can provide productive owl finding opportunities.

    1. Whiskered Screech and Elf Owls occur above the United States Forest Service's campground in the South Fork of Cave Creek Canyon, but the use of tape recorders here is prohibited.

    2. Spotted Owls occur fairly regularly in the main canyon below South Fork as well as in the South Fork of Cave Creek Canyon.

    3. Flammulated and Northern Pygmy Owls nest in Cave Creek Canyon and might be located if careful searches are made.
Access: From Portal, on the eastern side of the Chiricahua Mountains, drive 5 miles (8 kilometers) to Cave Creek Canyon and explore the area via vehicle and foot. Secure more detailed directions for reaching the canyon in Portal.

HUALAPAI MOUNTAIN PARK (near Kingman)

Owls Present: Flammulated.
Description: High, rugged mountains with ponderosa pine stands on the mountain slopes and deep, cold canyons with aspen, fir, and cottonwood. Flammulated Owls are common in the area.
Access: From Kingman drive south on Interstate 40 for 14 miles (22.4 kilometers) to East Kingman. There leave I-40 and follow signs to the park which can be explored on foot.

MADERA CANYON (near Tucson)

Owls Present: Western Screech, Whiskered Screech, Flammulated, Great Horned, Northern Pygmy, Elf, Spotted, and Long-eared.

Description: Oak forest in the vicinity of the Santa Rita Lodge where night owl watching/listening is very rewarding. **Access:** From Tucson drive south to Continental, turn left at a store and cross over railroad tracks, then continue for 7.0 miles (11.2 kilometers) to the junction with Box Canyon Road. Turn right and continue up into the canyon to the lodge from whose vicinity splendid night owl watching/listening is possible.

MOUNT LEMMON AREA (near Tucson)

Owls Present: Spotted.
Description: Dense growths of conifers in wooded canyons with streams provide roost sites for Spotted Owls when Great Horned Owls are not present in such areas. Spencer Canyon and Bear Wallow Campgrounds sometimes produce Spotted Owl sightings.
Access: From Tucson drive east on Tanque Verde Road for a few miles to Hitchcock Highway (Catalina Highway), then continue north on Hitchcock Highway for a number of miles to the respective campgrounds mentioned. Search for owls in those areas.

PHOENIX AREA

Owls Present: Common Barn, Western Screech, Burrowing, and Short-eared.
Description: Several locations in the Phoenix area provide owl finding opportunities including the following three sites.

1. Farmland—Alfalfa fields, on *private property* at 115th and Broadway Avenues and 123rd and Broadway Avenues, in which Common Barn and Burrowing Owls occur throughout the year and Short-eared Owls sometimes are seen from October through March. Owl watchers should confine their activities to the public roadside. From Phoenix drive south on lower Buckeye Road then turn south on 115th Avenue and continue for about 3 miles (4.8 kilometers) to Broadway Avenue.

2. Sewage Ponds—Vacant desert land with occasional saltbush and creosote bush on which Burrowing Owls live throughout the year. The ponds and surrounding area to the north, south, and east are located about 0.5 mile (0.8

kilometer) south of the intersection of Lower Buckeye Road and 35th Avenue in southwest Phoenix.

  3. Ranchland (private)—A grove of Giant Salt Cedars in which Common Barn and Western Screech Owls occur throughout the year. Owl watchers should not walk onto the ranch, but can confine their activities to the side of the public road. From the junction of Lower Buckeye Road and 51st Avenue, drive south for about 0.5 mile (0.8 kilometer) until the grove of cedars is encountered along the west side of the road.

Arkansas
JONESBORO

Owls Present: Short-eared.
Description: Grassy fields and other areas around the municipal airport. Short-eared Owls sometimes occur here in autumn.
Access: From the junction of U. S. Route 63 and State Route 1, on the south side of Jonesboro, drive north on State Route 1 to Nettleton Avenue, then continue east on Nettleton Avenue to Airport Road. Here cross the railroad tracks, and continue on Airport Road around the airport while searching open grassy areas for owls.

PINNACLE MOUNTAIN STATE PARK
(near Little Rock)

Owls Present: Eastern Screech, Great Horned, and Barred.
Description: A 1,354-acre park whose paved Kingfisher Trail loops for 0.5 mile (0.8 kilometer) through a picnic area along the Little Maumelle River's floodplain. Bald cypress, sweet gum, sycamore, river birch and other trees provide excellent habitat for Barred Owls which are commonly seen and heard during early morning and late afternoon hours. Benches along the trail provide excellent owl watching/listening stations, and the trail itself is suitable for use by persons confined to wheelchairs. Eastern Screech and Great Horned Owls are less common in the park.
Access: From Exit 9 off Interstate 430 on the western side of Little Rock, follow State Route 10 west for 7.0 miles (11.2 kilometers) to the junction with State Route 300. Turn onto State Route 300 and continue north for 2.0 miles (3.2

kilometers) to the park. Alternatively follow Pinnacle Valley
Road north off State Route 10 about 3.0 miles (4.8 kilometers)
west of Interstate 430. Maps and other park information can
be obtained at the park's Visitor Center. The park is open
daily between 6:00 a.m. and 10:00 p.m.

VILLAGE CREEK STATE PARK
(near Forrest City)

Owls Present: Eastern Screech, Great Horned, Barred, and
Short-eared.
Description: A 7,000 acre area on top of Crowley's Ridge, in
eastern Arkansas, in which rich deciduous woodland, two
lakes, and other suitable owl habitat provide owl watching/lis-
tening opportunities.
Access: From Forrest City drive east for a short distance on
Interstate 40 to Exit 242 and the junction with State Route
284. Turn onto State Route 284 and continue north for 12.0
miles (19.2 kilometers) to the park entrance. Ask at the Visitor
Center for additional owl watching/listening information.

WHITE RIVER NATIONAL WILDLIFE
REFUGE (near St. Charles)

Owls Present: Common Barn, Eastern Screech, Great Horned,
Barred, and Short-eared.
Description: A 116,302-acre refuge along a 65-mile section
of the White River in which bayous, chutes, channels, lakes,
forested areas, and fields provide suitable owl habitat. The
refuge's Farm Unit is best for owl watching/listening.
Access: From the junction of Routes 1 and 17 near St.
Charles, drive south on Route 17 for 3.0 miles (4.8 kilometers)
then east on a gravel road for about 1.5 miles (2.4 kilometers)
to the refuge's Farm Unit headquarters.

California
HUNT-WESSON HAWK AND OWL PRESERVE
(near Davis)

Owls Present: Common Barn, Short-eared, and Great Horned;
also Burrowing on rarer occasions.
Description: A 320-acre area consisting of undulating ditches
and cropland on which a series of sprinkler heads spray food

processing waste water. The sprinkler heads are used as hunting and feeding perches by the various birds of prey. Best viewing months are from late October to March.

Access: From Davis drive east on Route 80 to the Mace Boulevard exit. Take this exit and drive north on Mace Boulevard until it curves to the west and becomes Covell Boulevard. Remain on Covell Boulevard until you arrive at the stop sign at Road 102. Turn right onto Road 102 and continue north for about 3 miles (4.8 kilometers) to Road 28H. Turn right and continue east on Road 28H to the preserve located about a mile (1.6 kilometers) down the road on the north side. A fence prevents access to the property which is marked by a sign reading "Hawk and Owl Preserve—sponsored by Hunt-Wesson Foods, Inc." However, you can easily observe owls and other raptors by parking along Road 28H or on another road running along the eastern border of the preserve.

MOUNT PINOS (near Frazier Park)

Owls Present: Northern Pygmy, Flammulated, and Northern Saw-whet.

Description: The parking lot near the summit area of a 8,831-foot-high mountain is famous, during the day, as an observation lookout for California Condors, but is also useful at night for owl watching.

Access: From Los Angeles drive north on Interstate 5 (Golden State Freeway) for 64 miles (102.4 kilometers) through the town of Gorman and over the Tejon Pass to the Frazier Park off-ramp. This is the first off-ramp north of Gorman. Exit here and drive west for 6.8 miles (10.8 kilometers) through Frazier Park to Lake-of-the-Woods. When the road forks, follow the right fork and continue up Mt. Pinos road for 19 miles (30.4 kilometers). Ignore a junction with a right turn on the road. Instead, remain on the main road past the McGill and Mt. Pinos campgrounds (both excellent) to a large parking area where the road ends. Enter the parking area, then follow an unpaved road leading off the left side of the parking area for 1.5 miles (2.4 kilometers) to the paved parking lot at the condor observation point. Park and check (listen) for owls in the general area as well as elsewhere on Mount Pinos.

POINT LOBOS RESERVE STATE PARK
(near Carmel)

Owls Present: Northern Pygmy.
Description: Groves of cypresses, pines, and oaks through which trails penetrate. Northern Pygmy Owls sometimes can be heard inland in pine areas in the park.
Access: From Carmel, drive south on State Route 1 for a few miles to the park entrance where a map of the area may be obtained and other information secured.

SALTON SEA NATIONAL WILDLIFE REFUGE
(near Brawley)

Owls Present: Burrowing.
Description: A 36,527-acre area 230 feet below sea level in the Imperial Valley of southern California. Burrowing Owls sometimes are seen along State Route 111 and Sinclair Road as you approach the refuge headquarters.
Access: From Brawley drive north on State Route 111 to paved Sinclair Road, then turn left (west) onto Sinclair Road and continue for 5.6 miles (8.9 kilometers) to the refuge headquarters. Ask there for current information on the status of owls in the refuge and nearby areas.

SANTA YNEZ RECREATION AREA
(near Santa Ynez)

Owls Present: Western Screech, Great Horned, and Spotted (rare).
Description: A campground and park area in whose chaparral-oak woodland owls can be called up at night.
Access: From Santa Ynez seek local directions to the recreation area, drive there, and check and listen for owls at night by attempting to call them up.

SWITZER PICNIC AREA (near La Cañada)

Owls Present: Great Horned and Spotted.
Description: A streambed lined with oaks and sycamores, and chaparral on nearby slopes. Listen for owls and attempt to call them up.
Access: From Interstate 210 (Foothill Freeway) at La Cañada, turn onto State Route 2 (Angeles Crest Highway) and

continue for 12 miles (19.2 kilometers) to the Switzer Picnic Area at an elevation of 3,000 feet.

TOMALES BAY STATE PARK (near Olema)

Owls Present: Northern Pygmy, Spotted, and Northern Saw-whet.

Description: A 1,018-acre park in which owls can be heard but rarely seen.

Access: From Olema, drive north on State Route 1 then, just before Point Reyes Station, turn west onto Sir Francis Drake Boulevard and continue past Inverness to Pierce Point Road. Turn onto Pierce Point Road and continue for 2 miles (3.2 kilometers) to the entrance to Tomales Bay State Park. Search the area carefully, listening for owls.

YOSEMITE NATIONAL PARK (near Merced)

Owls Present: Great Horned, Northern Pygmy, Spotted, Great Gray, and Northern Saw-whet.

Description: A spectacular natural area with scenic valleys and mountains ranging in elevation from 4,000 feet on the valley floor to thousands of feet higher in the mountains. Great Horned, Northern Pygmy, Spotted, and Northern Saw-whet Owls occur in the valley, whereas the spectacular Great Gray Owl can be seen early in the morning or late in the evening along the wooded edges of Westfall Meadow as it perches in trees looking for prey in the open meadow.

Access: When inside the park continue to Bridalveil Campground via the Glacier Point Road, then hike on the trail from the campground to Westfall Meadow to try to observe Great Gray Owls. Also seek additional owl finding information from park rangers at information centers or headquarters. To reach the park from Merced, drive northeast on State Route 140 for 84 miles (134.4 kilometers) to the Arch Rock Entrance.

Colorado

CHERRY CREEK RESERVOIR STATE RECREATION AREA (near Denver)

Owls Present: Burrowing and Short-eared.

Description: A prairie dog colony in which one or more Burrowing Owls can be seen in summer. In winter look for Short-eared Owls in the area.

Access: From Denver drive south on Interstate 25 to Exit 90, about 10 miles (16 kilometers) from Denver, at which point leave Interstate 90 and turn left onto Belleview Avenue. Continue on that road for 1.5 miles (2.4 kilometers) to Dayton Avenue, turn left and continue on Dayton Avenue for about 1.5 miles (2.4 kilometers) past the entrance to the reservoir area. There look for the prairie dog colony on the right—and Burrowing Owls standing on top of the mounds or looking out from the rims of the holes.

PIKE NATIONAL FOREST (near Woodland Park)

Owls Present: Flammulated, Great Horned.
Description: The pine forest area near Colorado Campground and the nearby Manitou Lake Picnic Grounds. In summer, look in old flicker holes in aspen groves for Flammulated Owls.
Access: From Woodland Park follow U. S. Route 24 west to its junction with State Route 67, then continue north on State Route 67 for 6.9 miles (11 kilometers) to the Colorado Campground within Pike National Forest. To visit the Manitou Lake Picnic Grounds follow State Route 67 north for another 1.5 miles (2.4 kilometers) to the picnic grounds. Check both areas for owls.

SAN LUIS VALLEY (near Alamosa)

Owls Present: Great Horned, Long-eared, and Short-eared.
Description: A high, arid valley extending for 150 miles (240 kilometers) from Poncha Pass southward to New Mexico. Check any likely owl habitats for these birds.
Access: From Alamosa drive along any of the valley roads and make stops at likely owl habitats.

WETMORE AREA

Owls Present: Northern Pygmy.
Description: Utility wires along State Route 96 between Wetmore and Westcliffe. Look for Northern Pygmy Owls, in winter, perched on wires.
Access: From Wetmore drive west on State Route 96 toward Westcliffe.

Connecticut

BARN ISLAND WILDLIFE MANAGEMENT AREA (near Stonington)

Owls Present: Snowy and Short-eared.
Description: Freshwater and saltwater marshes, ponds, fields, and upland woodland. Owl watching is best done in winter.
Access: From Stonington drive east on State Route 1 for about 1.0 mile (1.6 kilometers) to the junction with State Route 1A. Turn right onto Palmer Neck Road, and continue another 1.7 miles (2.7 kilometers) to a boat ramp. Park, then explore on foot the nearby habitats of the management area opposite the parking lot.

CAMPBELL FALLS STATE PARK (near Norfolk)

Owls Present: Great Horned and Barred.
Description: A waterfall surrounded by deciduous and coniferous forest.
Access: From the junction of Routes 272 and 44 in Norfolk, drive north on Route 272 for 4.0 miles (6.4 kilometers) to Spaulding Road on the left. Turn onto Spaulding Road and continue for 0.2 mile (0.3 kilometer) to a parking area at a picnic area. Park and explore the surrounding areas on foot looking for owls. Trails lead throughout parts of the park.

DEVIL'S HOPYARD STATE PARK (near East Haddam)

Owls Present: Eastern Screech, Great Horned, and Barred.
Description: Wooded hillsides of a ravine on which owls nest.
Access: From Exit 70 of Interstate 95, near East Haddam, drive north on Route 156 for 8.7 miles (13.9 kilometers) to the junction with Route 82. Turn right onto Route 82 and continue another 0.2 mile (0.3 kilometer) to an unmarked road on the left. Turn left onto that road and continue for 3.3 miles (5.2 kilometers) to the park entrance. Enter, then park in a suitable area. Explore the evergreen forests on the surrounding hillsides on foot looking and listening for owls.

GUILFORD SLUICE (near Guilford)

Owls Present: Great Horned Owl, Long-eared, and Northern Saw-whet.

Description: Woodlots near the side of a marsh. Great Horned and Long-eared Owls roost in conifers in autumn and winter. Northern Saw-whet Owls are observed less frequently.

Access: From Interstate 95 (Connecticut Turnpike) near Guilford, turn off at Exit 59 (Goose Lane) and continue a short distance to a traffic light at Route 1. Cross Route 1 and continue a short distance to a blinking light at Seaview Road. Turn right onto Seaview and continue 0.6 mile (0.9 kilometer) to South Union Street. Turn left onto South Union and continue on that street to the point where it meets Saw Pit Road. Follow Saw Pit a short distance to railroad tracks. Park there and walk to the woodlots to listen or look for owls.

HAMMONASSET STATE PARK (near Madison)

Owls Present: Common Barn, Eastern Screech, Great Horned, Snowy, Barred, Long-eared, and Northern Saw-whet.

Description: Thick stands of cedar trees immediately north of a water tank in the northern part of the park. Autumn is particularly good for owl watching. During Snowy Owl invasion years these birds also are likely to be seen on the park's beach.

Access: Take Exit 62 from Interstate 95 (Connecticut Turnpike) and drive south on the so-called Hammonasset Connector to its junction with Route 1. Cross Route 1 and enter the park, then continue to the cedars or the beach within the park.

HOUSATONIC RIVER ROAD (near Kent)

Owls Present: Eastern Screech, Great Horned, Barred, and Northern Saw-whet.

Description: A 1.5 mile (2.4 kilometer) section of road running beside the Housatonic River.

Access: From the junction of Routes 7 and 341 in Kent, drive west on Route 341 and cross the bridge over the Housatonic River. At the far end of the bridge, turn left on Skiff Mountain Road and follow it for 1.0 mile (1.6 kilometers) to River Road which branches to the right. Follow River Road along the river for the next 1.5 miles (2.4 kilometers). Explore the wooded hillsides beside the river and road for owl nests.

MIANUS RIVER PARK (near Greenwich)

Owls Present: Eastern Screech and Barred.
Description: Wet woodland, field, rocky outcropping, swampland and other wetland, and the Mianus River. Foot trails penetrate many areas of the park. Best owl watching is reported during autumn and spring.
Access: Driving south on Interstate 95, leave that highway at Exit 4 (Indian Field Road). Turn right and follow Indian Field Road for 0.6 mile (0.9 kilometer) to its junction with Route 1. Continue through the traffic light and, turning right, turn left onto the next road which is Stanwhich Road. Continue for 3.6 miles (5.7 kilometers) on Stanwhich Road to Cognewaugh Road, turn right onto Cognewaugh, and drive another 0.5 mile (0.8 kilometer) to a parking lot on the left. Park, then walk along the trail leading into the park.

NEHANTIC STATE FOREST (near Lyme)

Owls Present: Barred.
Description: Woodland bordering a stream in the vicinity of a picnic area north of Uncas Lake.
Access: From Exit 70 of Interstate 95 (Connecticut Turnpike) turn left onto Route 156 and drive 3.8 miles (6 kilometers) to the forest entrance. Turn into the forest and continue 1.9 miles (3 kilometers) to the picnic area. Park and explore the surrounding woodland for Barred Owls which occasionally can be heard calling in mid-day.

WATERFORD BEACH (near New London)

Owls Present: Snowy and Short-eared.
Description: A large salt marsh attractive to Short-eared Owls. In winter, Snowy Owls also sometimes appear.
Access: From Interstate 95, turn onto State Route 213 and continue roughly 5 miles (8 kilometers) to Waterford Beach located east of Harkness Memorial State Park. Scan the marsh with binoculars for owls.

WHITE MEMORIAL FOUNDATION
(near Litchfield)

Owls Present: Great Horned and Barred.

Description: A 4,000-acre nature preserve containing varied habitats, excellent nature trails, and a fine nature center. Full details on owl watching on the property can be obtained from the nature center staff.

Access: From Litchfield drive south on Route 202 toward Bantam. Look for the foundation sign on the left side of the road. Enter the preserve there and continue to the nature center to seek full current information, maps of the area, and other literature.

Delaware

BLACKBIRD CREEK (near Port Penn)

Owls Present: Eastern Screech and Great Horned.

Description: Moist, wooded valleys in which two branches of Blackbird Creek flow.

Access: From Port Penn drive south on State Route 9 for about 9.9 miles (15.8 kilometers) to the junction with Route 456. Turn right onto Route 456 and continue to two points along the road where it crosses branches of Blackbird Creek—one near a house, the other at a wooden bridge. Check for owls at either spot.

LITTLE CREEK WILDLIFE AREA (near Dover)

Owls Present: Eastern Screech, Great Horned, Barred, Short-eared, and Northern Saw-whet.

Description: A wetland and surrounding areas. The Port Mahon Road tidal area north of the road produces Short-eared Owl viewing opportunities during winter. Northern Saw-whet Owls sometimes are found in holly vegetation near Pickering Beach in winter. Night owl watching/listening forays along this same road in summer can produce sounds of Eastern Screech, Great Horned, and Barred Owls.

Access: From Dover drive east on State Route 8 for 4.5 miles (7.2 kilometers) to State Route 9. Turn south (right) and follow Route 9 for 0.4 mile (0.6 kilometer) then turn left onto Port Mahon Road (Road 89) leading to the Little Creek

Wildlife Area. To reach the Pickering Beach road drive south on State Route 9 for 0.9 mile (1.4 kilometers) then turn onto the next road left (Road 349) and continue 2.1 miles (3.3 kilometers) to Pickering Beach.

Florida
CORKSCREW SWAMP SANCTUARY
(near Immokalee)

Owls Present: Barred.
Description: A virgin bald cypress stand through which a mile of boardwalk loops providing visitors with easy access to the interior of the swamp. Owls sometimes are seen or heard from various sections of the boardwalk.
Access: From Immokalee drive west on State Route 846 for 16 miles (25.6 kilometers) to the sanctuary entrance. A small admission fee is charged by the National Audubon Society which owns and operates the sanctuary.

CROOM WILDLIFE MANAGEMENT AREA
(near Brooksville)

Owls Present: Barred.
Description: Hammock, oak ridge, and cypress forest bordering Silver Lake—a wide section of the Withlacoochee River. Barred Owls are heard frequently in the area.
Access: From Brooksville turn east onto U. S. Route 98 and continue for 10.1 miles (16.1 kilometers) to unmarked State Route 39 beyond a railroad overpass. Turn left onto State Route 39 and follow it for 3.7 miles (5.9 kilometers) to an unpaved road going to Silver Lake. Turn and continue to the lake where owl watching/listening is possible.

ESCAMBIA RIVER SWAMP (near Pensacola)

Owls Present: Eastern Screech, Great Horned, and Barred.
Description: A causeway crossing the Escambia River swamp from which owls can be heard at night.
Access: From the junction of U. S. Route 29 and State Route 95A near Pensacola, drive south on State Route 95A to its junction with State Route 184. Turn onto State Route 184 and continue east to the causeway across the Escambia River swamp. Park in a suitable spot, and listen for owls at night.

EVERGLADES NATIONAL PARK
(near Homestead)

Owls Present: Barred.
Description: Tropical vegetation in Royal Palm and Mahogany Hammocks. Owls can be heard from time to time in both sites.
Access: From Homestead follow State Route 27 southwest for 12 miles (19.2 kilometers) to the park entrance. Stop at the visitor center inside the park for maps and other information.

KISSIMMEE PRAIRIE (near Kenansville)

Owls Present: Burrowing.
Description: Prairies on which palmettos, sparce grasses, and other vegetation grows. Burrowing Owls are found in various portions of the Kissimmee Prairie.
Access: From Kenansville drive southwest on an unpaved road for some 6 to 8 miles (9.6 to 12.8 kilometers) to various prairies on which owls are found nesting in burrows. Such birds should be observed from safe distances so they are not disturbed.

LAKE PLACID AREA

Owls Present: Burrowing.
Description: A large colony of Burrowing Owls in a pasture near a road.
Access: At the junction of U. S. Route 27 and Route 621, drive east on Route 621 to a very large barn on the east side of the road. Stop there and look across the road to a pasture in which a Burrowing Owl colony is located. Do not approach the birds on foot.

MOUNTAIN LAKE SANCTUARY
(near Lake Wales)

Owls Present: Common Barn and Eastern Screech.
Description: A 117-acre sanctuary on Iron Mountain. Common Barn Owls nest in a box on a high tower, and Eastern Screech Owls use a box placed on a tree.
Access: The sanctuary is located 3 miles (4.8 kilometers) north of Lake Wales on the slope of Iron Mountain. Secure additional directions in the vicinity of the sanctuary.

MYAKKA RIVER STATE PARK (near Sarasota)

Owls Present: Barred.
Description: A 28,874-acre park where Barred Owls can be heard near the entrance at night.
Access: From Sarasota drive south on U. S. Route 41 for 3 miles (4.8 kilometers) to State Route 72. Turn west onto Route 72 and drive 14 miles (22.4 kilometers) to the park entrance.

REEDY CREEK (near Kissimmee)

Owls Present: Great Horned and Barred.
Description: A creek in whose vicinity owls can be heard early in the morning or in the evening.
Access: From Kissimmee drive south on U. S. Routes 17 and 92 to the junction with State Route 531. Turn left (south) onto State Route 531 and continue ahead for more than 5 miles (8 kilometers) to the bridge crossing Reedy Creek. Park in a suitable spot and check the area for owls.

ROCK SPRINGS PARK (near Apopka)

Owls Present: Barred.
Description: An oak-hickory-pine woodland and stream in which Barred Owls occur in winter.
Access: From Apopka drive north on State Route 435 for 5.5 miles (8.8 kilometers) to the park.

VACA KEY

Owls Present: Burrowing.
Description: Areas beside a golf course where owls live.
Access: At mile marker 50 on U. S. Route 1 across the Florida Keys look for the Marathon State Bank. From there continue south to the first road past the 50 mile marker, then turn left and drive around the edge of the Sombrero Beach Club's Golf Course. Watch for owls on the ground during spring and summer, or perched in Australian Pines around the course.

Georgia

OKEFENOKEE SWAMP (near Fargo)

Owls Present: Barred and Eastern Screech.

Description: A splendid 700-square-mile wilderness swamp and marsh near the Florida border. Barred and Screech Owls are common nesting birds in the swamp, and almost every boat trip into the interior of the area produces an owl, or family of them, along the Fargo side of the swamp. Alternatively, Barred and Eastern Screech Owls also can sometimes be found along almost any road through or along the edge of the swamp.

Access: From Fargo drive northeast on State Route 177 for about 18 miles (28.8 kilometers) to the Stephen C. Foster State Park entrance to the swamp. Obtain information there on the availability of boats and guides into Okefenokee, or roads leading through or around the swamp.

Idaho
LEMHI RIVER VALLEY AREA (near Salmon)

Owls Present: Short-eared.

Description: A wide, flat, river valley with extensive woodlands, thickets, pastures, and irrigated fields. Look for Short-eared Owls in open areas near the road.

Access: From Salmon, drive southeast on State Route 28 for 45 miles (72 kilometers) to Leadore, looking for owls along the way.

SNAKE RIVER BIRDS OF PREY NATURAL AREA (near Boise)

Owls Present: Common Barn, Western Screech, Great Horned, Burrowing, and Long-eared.

Description: A unique 31,000-acre natural area containing rugged river canyons and cliffs which provide nest sites for large numbers of hawks, eagles, falcons along 33 miles (52.8 kilometers) of the Snake River in southwestern Idaho. The area is noted for impressive numbers of nesting Golden Eagles and Prairie Falcons, but numerous owls also inhabit the area.

Access: From Boise, Idaho, drive west on U. S. Route 30 to Meridan, then continue south on State Route 69 to Kuna. From Kuna drive south for about 18 miles (28.8 kilometers) on the Swan Falls Road to Swan Falls within the Birds of Prey Natural Area. Various roads also run through the area.

Circulars and maps, along with additional information, are available from the Manager, Birds of Prey Natural Area, Bureau of Land Management, 230 Collins Road, Boise, Idaho 83702.

Illinois

CARPENTER PARK (near Springfield)

Owls Present: Barred.
Description: A 438-acre forest preserve in which Barred Owls nest.
Access: From Springfield drive north on U. S. Business Route 66 for 4.0 miles (6.4 kilometers) to a bridge over the Sangamon River. Cross the bridge, take the first left turn, and drive to the picnic area. Park and explore the area on foot by following the trails leading through the park.

CHICAGO AREA

Owls Present: Snowy and Short-eared.
Description: Open areas around Meigs Field Airport on the lakefront off of the Lake Shore Drive opposite the Field Museum of Natural History northward to Montrose Harbor. Snowy Owls sometimes appear from early October through late March, especially early in December, on pilings, break-waters, ice, and other structures along the lake.
Access: In Chicago drive to Lake Shore Drive and search the lakefront between Meigs Field (1400 South) to Montrose Harbor (4400 North). Additional details on owl watching in the Chicago area may be available from the Chicago Audubon Hotline.

CRAB ORCHARD NATIONAL WILDLIFE REFUGE (near Carbondale)

Owls Present: Great Horned and Barred.
Description: A 43,017-acre refuge in southern Illinois in which Great Horned Owls and Barred Owls nest.
Access: From Carbondale drive east on State Route 13 for 11.0 miles (17.6 kilometers), then south on State Route 148 to the refuge entrance. Seek additional information on owl watching/listening at the refuge information center or office.

FOREST GLEN COUNTY PRESERVE
(near Danville)

Owls Present: Eastern Screech, Great Horned, Barred, and Short-eared.

Description: A 1,800-acre natural area. Look or listen for Eastern Screech, Great Horned, and Barred Owls year around; in winter Short-eared Owls may appear.

Access: From Danville leave Interstate 74 at the Westville Exit and drive south on State Route 1 to Georgetown. Turn east on Mill Street and continue another 6.0 miles (9.6 kilometers) following preserve signs to the entrance. A map of the area is available at the visitor center, and additional birding and owl watching/listening information can be obtained at the Willow Shores Nature Center.

LINCOLN'S NEW SALEM STATE PARK
(near Petersburg)

Owls Present: Great Horned.

Description: A hill overlooking a river valley. Best owl finding is done later in spring and early in summer.

Access: From Springfield drive north on State Route 97 for about 20 miles (32 kilometers) to the park.

PÈRE MARQUETTE STATE PARK
(near Grafton)

Owls Present: Barred.

Description: An 8,000-acre park in which Barred Owls nest regularly and can be seen and/or heard.

Access: From Grafton drive west on State Route 100 for 6.5 miles (10.4 kilometers) to the park entrance on the right.

Indiana
INDIANA DUNES NATIONAL LAKESHORE AREA

Owls Present: Snowy.

Description: Ice floes along the Lake Michigan shore. Check floes and shore in winter for an occasional Snowy Owl.

Access: Follow State Route 12 along the Lake Michigan shore between Gary and Michigan City.

PIONEER MOTHERS MEMORIAL FOREST
(near Paoli)

Owls Present: Great Horned and Barred.
Description: A 254-acre forest of which 116 acres are virgin hardwoods.
Access: From Paoli drive south from the courthouse on State Route 37 for 2.1 miles (3.3 kilometers) to the Pioneer Mothers Rest Park, or follow U.S. Route 150 east for 1.3 miles (2 kilometers) then turn right onto the paved entrance road and drive to the parking area. Trails from both locations allow exploration of the forest. The latter road is open from April through mid-October.

Iowa

CREDIT ISLAND PARK (near Davenport)

Owls Present: Barred.
Description: A 420-acre park whose southern end has excellent bottomland forest in which Barred Owls occur and may be heard or perhaps seen.
Access: From Interstate 280, to the west of Davenport, drive east (marked north) on U. S. Route 61 for 3.5 miles (5.6 kilometers), then turn right at a park sign and continue to the park.

EAGLE POINT PARK (in Clinton)

Owls Present: Barred.
Description: A grove of pines near a stone tower in a 121-acre park on bluffs overlooking the Mississippi River. Owls sometimes occur in the pines.
Access: In Clinton, turn east from U. S. Route 67 (North 3rd Street) into the park. In winter Eagle Point Park is closed to automobiles, but bird watchers can walk into the park and look for birds.

STONE STATE PARK (in Sioux City)

Owls Present: Eastern Screech, Great Horned, and Barred.
Description: A 1,200-acre park whose bluffs and valleys are located on the east bank of the Big Sioux River. Wooded valleys, and dense shrub thickets on the slopes, should be

searched carefully for owls which often can be heard more easily than seen.

Access: From Interstate 29 at Sioux City, drive north on State Route 12 (Riverside Boulevard) for 3 miles (4.8 kilometers) to the park entrance in the 4000 block of Stone Park Boulevard.

TIEG'S MARSH (near Story City)

Owls Present: Short-eared.

Description: A small, shallow marsh surrounded by some pasture and upland areas. During many years, from late autumn to spring, owls can be observed at dusk from nearby roads.

Access: From Ames drive north on Interstate 35 to Exit 124 (Story City), leave I-35 there, and drive west a relatively short distance to Story City. From there drive west for about 0.5 mile (0.8 kilometer) to U. S. Route 69, then continue north on Route 69 for about 0.5 mile (0.8 kilometer) to a blacktop road. Turn left (west) onto the blacktop road and continue about 3.0 miles (4.8 kilometers) to a gravel road. Turn right (north) onto the gravel road and continue a short distance looking for the marsh on the right. Observe from the road but do not enter the marsh and surrounding land which is private property.

Kansas

ARGONIA AREA (near Wellington)

Owls Present: Great Horned and Burrowing.

Description: Almost every large woodlot, in close proximity to rivers, produces horned owls within a 15-mile radius of the town of Argonia. Similarly, Burrowing Owls sometimes inhabit prairie dog towns in the area. Check such towns at dusk for the presence of these birds.

Access: Argonia is located on U. S. Route 160 about 20 miles (32 kilometers) west of Wellington. From Argonia drive along rural roads in the vicinity of the town and attempt to call up horned owls at various woodlots. To see Burrowing Owls, drive north from Argonia on the Argonia-Suppesville Road to a prairie dog town on the west side of the road. Up to seven owls have been seen in this town.

CHEYENNE BOTTOMS STATE WILDLIFE MANAGEMENT AREA (near Great Bend)

Owls Present: Snowy (in winter) and Burrowing.
Description: A series of shallow pools, dikes, marsh, wet meadow, sandy plain, swampy woodland, and pastures. Burrowing Owls occur around prairie dog towns in the area, and their current locations and status can be obtained at the refuge headquarters. During some winters, Snowy Owls occur on the barren wastes of the Cheyenne Bottoms and should be searched for carefully. *Caution*—remain alert for Massasauga Rattlesnakes which are not uncommon along roadsides and in thick, dry, grassy areas close to water.
Access: From the junction of U. S. Routes 56 and 281, drive north on U. S. Route 281 for 5 miles (8 kilometers), then turn east on a marked gravel road and continue for another 2 miles (3.2 kilometers) to the refuge headquarters. There you can get information on owl finding as well as other bird watching details.

Kentucky

KLEBER WILDLIFE AREA (near Frankfort)

Owls Present: Great Horned.
Description: A 685-acre wooded tract.
Access: From Frankfort drive north on U. S. Route 127 for a few miles to the junction with State Route 368. Turn right (east) onto Route 368 and continue a few miles to the wildlife area. Listen for, or attempt to call up, owls in the area.

MAMMOTH CAVE NATIONAL PARK (near Cave City)

Owls Present: Eastern Screech, Great Horned, and Barred.
Description: An original and second-growth woodland.
Access: From the Cave City exit of Interstate 65 drive west on State Route 70 for 8 miles (12.8 kilometers) to the park border, then cross Mammoth Cave Ridge to the headquarters at Mammoth Cave. Road and trail maps are available here. After securing these aids, drive north from the headquarters to the store at Ollie just north and west of the park. Listen for owls here at night.

Louisiana
PEARL RIVER WILDLIFE MANAGEMENT AREA (near New Orleans)

Owls Present: Barred.

Description: A 27,000-acre section of tupelo-cypress swamp bottoms near the Mississippi border. Listen for Barred Owls from roads adjacent to the swamps or attempt to call the birds.

Access: From New Orleans, drive northeast on Interstate 10 for about 16 miles (25.6 kilometers) to the junction with Interstate 59. Then continue northeast on I-59 for 6 miles (9.6 kilometers), go across the West Pearl River, and leave I-59 at Ext 5B (Honey Island Swamp Exit). Follow the paved road (formerly U. S. Route 11) to the East Pearl River, or turn from the road before reaching the river onto either of two gravel roads and follow them for several miles. Make stops along the way listening for owls.

Maine
BACK COVE (in Portland)

Owls Present: Snowy.

Description: A field just beyond a large parking area in which Snowy Owls sometimes are seen from late November to March. Look elsewhere along Back Cove for owls as well.

Access: From the junction of Interstate 295 and U. S. Route 302/State Route 100 (Forest Avenue) drive north on U. S. Route 302 to the Baxter Boulevard exit. Then turn onto Baxter Boulevard and follow it as it circles around the back of Back Cove to the parking area.

FLETCHER NECK AREA (near Biddeford)

Owls Present: Snowy and Short-eared.

Description: A golf course at the East Point end of Fletcher Neck where Snowy and Short-eared Owls sometimes occur during winter.

Access: From Exit 5 of the Maine Turnpike near Biddeford, drive into town, cross U. S. Route 1, then turn right onto Route 9 (Main Street). Follow Route 9 across the Saco River, turn left at a gentle turn onto Hill Street, then continue 0.3 miles (0.4 kilometers) to a traffic light. Turn left onto Routes 9 and

208 (Pool Street) and drive 5.5 miles (8.8 kilometers) to the junction with Route 208. Turn left onto Route 208 and continue out Fletcher Neck to the East Point area and the golf course. Check that area for owls.

POPHAM BEACH STATE PARK (south of Bath)

Owls Present: Snowy.
Description: Marshland and beach on which Snowy Owls may occur during winter.
Access: Some 12 miles (19.2 kilometers) south of Bath on Route 209. Signs clearly mark the park's entrance.

RACHEL CARSON NATIONAL WILDLIFE REFUGE (near Wells)

Owls Present: Snowy and Short-eared.
Description: One of several units of the refuge located along coastal Maine. Snowy and Short-eared Owls sometimes occur on marshland during winter.
Access: From Kittery or other points in southern Maine, drive north on Interstate 95 to the Wells Exit (east and south). Leave I-95 there and follow Route 109 for about 1.5 miles (2.4 kilometers) eastward toward Wells to the junction with U. S. Route 1. Turn north onto U. S. Route 1 and continue 1.9 miles (3 kilometers). Then turn right (east) onto Route 9 and continue for about 0.7 miles (1.1 kilometers) to the refuge entrance. Look for owls in the refuge marshland.

SCARBOROUGH MARSH (near West Scarborough)

Owls Present: Snowy.
Description: A marsh, nature center, and wildlife management area on which Snowy Owls may occur during winter.
Access: From the junction of U. S. Route 1 and Route 9 in West Scarborough, drive southeast on Route 9 (Pine Point Road) checking the nearby marsh for owls. Stop at the Scarborough Marsh Nature Center along Route 9 for the latest owl (and other birding) information.

WESKEAG MARSH (in South Thomaston)

Owls Present: Barred and Snowy.

Description: Marshland, fields, and woodland. During winter Barred and Snowy Owls may occur in the area.
Access: In Thomaston follow Buttermilk Lane, east of the Martin-Marietta Cement Plant, toward South Thomaston. After 1.0 mile (1.6 kilometers), at a road dip, note the marsh on the right. Continue another 0.4 miles (0.6 kilometers) to a ridge from which you can scan the marsh.

Maryland

BLACK BOTTOM ROAD (near Massey)

Owls Present: Eastern Screech, Great Horned, Barred, and Northern Saw-whet (rare).
Description: A rural area in which owls sometimes can be seen or heard.
Access: From the junction of U. S. Route 301 and State Route 313, near Massey, turn east onto State Route 313 and continue to the town of Massey. Once there continue straight ahead for another 3.2 miles (5.1 kilometers) to Black Bottom Road. Turn left onto that road and make frequent stops to listen for, or call up, owls.

EASTERN NECK NATIONAL WILDLIFE REFUGE (near Rock Hall)

Owls Present: Eastern Screech, Great Horned, Barred, Short-eared, and Northern Saw-whet.
Description: A 2,285-acre refuge on the Eastern Shore containing varied habitat including wooded areas and marshland.
Access: From Rock Hall drive south on State Route 445 for about 6 miles (10.8 kilometers) to a bridge, then cross the bridge onto an island where the refuge is located. Owl watching must be done only from the road at night, but wooded areas near the road can produce birds. In winter, Short-eared Owls also sometimes are seen over the marshland on the island.

MIDDLE PATUXENT VALLEY (near Columbia)

Owls Present: Common Barn, Eastern Screech, and Barred year around; Great Horned, Long-eared, and Northern Saw-whet sometimes appear in winter.

Description: An unspoiled natural area in western Columbia.
Access: The area is located between State Routes 108 and 32 west of Columbia.

PERKINS HILL ROAD (near Kennedyville)

Owls Present: Barred.
Description: A rural area where owls can sometimes be heard.
Access: From Kennedyville, on the Eastern Shore, drive south on State Route 213 for 2.2 miles (3.5 kilometers) to Perkins Hill Road. Turn left onto that road and continue to the first double culvert from where it's possible to listen for, or call up, Barred Owls.

ROCK HILL AREA

Owls Present: Eastern Screech, Great Horned, and Barred.
Description: Wooded areas in the vicinity of Rock Hall, on the Eastern Shore, especially along State Route 445 from Rock Hall southward to Eastern Neck National Wildlife Refuge.
Access: From Rock Hall drive south on State Route 445 and stop at wooded areas well away from homes to listen for owls, or attempt to call them.

Massachusetts
GOOSEBERRY NECK (near Fall River)

Owls Present: Snowy, and Short-eared.
Description: A peninsula on which Short-eared Owls frequently are reported in autumn, and occasionally Snowy Owls in winter.
Access: From Fall River drive east on Interstate 195 for a few miles to the junction with State Route 88, then continue south on Route 88 to the point where this highway becomes John Reed Road. Continue on John Reed Road to the ocean, then right over a causeway to Gooseberry Neck. Park and explore the area, remaining alert for Short-eared Owls in autumn and an occasional Snowy Owl in winter.

MARTHA'S VINEYARD

Owls Present: Short-eared.
Description: An island off Cape Cod with varied habitats. In winter, Short-eared Owls can be seen in various parts of the island.
Access: Via ferry from Woods Hole on the Massachusetts mainland. Various roads cross the island thus allowing owl watchers access to much of the island.

NANTUCKET

Owls Present: Short-eared.
Description: An island off Cape Cod on which Short-eared Owls appear in summer.
Access: Via ferry from Woods Hole. Roads on the island allow exploration of likely owl sites by bird watchers.

PLUM ISLAND (near Newburyport)

Owls Present: Great Horned, Snowy, Long-eared, Short-eared, and Northern Saw-whet.
Description: A barrier beach island, about 8 miles (12.8 kilometers) long, containing ocean beach, dune complexes, salt meadows, freshwater pools, and adjacent dikes. The lower two-thirds of the island forms the Parker River National Wildlife Refuge. Snowy Owls, often seen from late autumn to early spring, and Short-eared Owls occasionally seen hunting over open areas, are the most likely species of owls to be encountered on the island.
Access: From Newburyport follow Water Street east to the Plum Island Turnpike then continue east on that road to Plum Island. Once on the island drive south on Sunset Boulevard to the southern tip, looking for owls and other birds along the way.

Michigan
WHITEFISH POINT

Owls Present: Long-eared, Boreal, Northern Saw-whet; Great Gray (rarely).
Description: The general vicinity of the lighthouse, parking lot, or dunes along the shoreline of Lake Superior. April and

May are especially productive months for finding Boreal and Northern Saw-whet Owls.

Access: From the Lower Peninsula cross the Straits of Mackinac on Interstate 75 and continue northward to the junction of Route 123. Turn onto Route 123 and continue north to Paradise. Then follow an unnumbered road north for about 12 miles (19.2 kilometers) to Whitefish Point.

Minnesota
AITKIN AREA

Owls Present: Great Horned, Snowy, Northern Hawk, Barred, Great Gray, and Short-eared.

Description: A low, flat area containing spruce and tamarac bogs, open fields, and rice paddies. Best owl watching is done during winter and early spring.

Access: From Aitkin drive north on Aitkin County Road 1 for about 13.5 miles (21.6 kilometers). En route explore likely spots for owls, including looking for birds perched near the road. In addition, explore side roads leading east off of the county road for additional owl watching opportunities. The Aitkin area is one of Minnesota's better owl watching locations.

BELTRAMI ISLAND STATE FOREST AREA (near Roseau)

Owls Present: Snowy, Northern Hawk, and Great Gray.

Description: A wild, remote forested area in whose vicinity various northern owls may be discovered, in winter, along roadsides or elsewhere.

Access: From Roseau drive south on State Route 89 for 15 miles (24 kilometers) then turn left (east) onto another road and continue for about 8 miles (12.8 kilometers) to the park entrance. Explore various roads in the vicinity of the state forest.

DULUTH

Owls Present: Snowy, Great Gray, and Boreal.

Description: The city's harbor area and the shoreline of Lake Superior between Duluth and Two Harbors. In winter, Snowy Owls are most likely to be discovered, but occasionally other rare northern owls also appear.

Access: At the junction of Interstate Routes 35 and 535 follow Interstate 535 right toward Superior, Wisconsin. Leave I-535 at the first Port Terminal exit, just before crossing the large bridge. After taking the Port Terminal exit follow the street on which you are driving as it passes along the harbor. Make frequent stops to search for Snowy Owls or other species.

HASTINGS AREA

Owls Present: Long-eared, Short-eared, and Northern Saw-whet.
Description: Fields and river bottom woodland in which winter owl watching may be productive at potential roost sites or during owl listening at night.
Access: In Hastings drive south on U. S. Route 61 to County Route 54 at 10th Street. Turn left onto County Route 54 and follow it as it passes along the Vermillion River toward Etter. En route stop at likely owl roosts or hunting areas and check for birds.

MEADOWLANDS AREA

Owls Present: Northern Hawk and Great Gray.
Description: A series of rural roads crossing the Sax-Zim Bog. In winter Northern Hawk Owls, and more rarely Great Gray Owls, sometimes are seen perched on trees or utility poles in the general area of the town of Meadowlands.
Access: From Floodwood drive north on State Route 73 for 2.0 miles (3.2 kilometers) to the junction with County Route 29. Turn right (east) onto County Route 29 and follow it northeastward to the edge of the town of Meadowlands. En route remain alert for Northern Hawk Owls, or other northern owls, beside the road. Explore other roads in the Meadowlands area, too, paying attention to the tops of poles and trees for perched birds.

NORTH SHORE OF LAKE SUPERIOR
(north of Duluth)

Owls Present: Boreal.
Description: A scenic highway along which Boreal Owls sometimes are seen in winter as they perch on signs, poles, posts, or other objects beside the road.
Access: From Duluth, drive northeast on State Route 61

(North Shore Highway) for 21 miles (33.6 kilometers) to Two Harbors. Check all likely perches along the way for these small owls.

RED LAKE WILDLIFE MANAGEMENT AREA (near Baudette)

Owls Present: Northern Hawk, Great Gray, and Boreal.
Description: A northern coniferous forest, 427,570 acres in size, in which various northern owls sometimes appear in winter beside roads where they perch on poles, wires, posts, trees, and other elevated objects.
Access: From Baudette, drive west on State Route 11 for 20 miles (32 kilometers) to Roosevelt. There turn south onto State Forest Service Road and continue about 15 miles (24 kilometers) to a headquarters area at "Norris Camp" where the latest owl finding information may be available. Because of the remote and wild nature of this country, care should be taken not to venture deep into forest without adequate equipment and a compass.

ROSEAU AREA

Owls Present: Snowy, Northern Hawk, and Great Gray.
Description: Wild, remote spruce bogs and conifer forest in which rare northern owls may appear in winter along roadsides where trees, poles, wires, and other perches are used. Great Gray Owls are possible finds.
Access: From Roseau drive north on State Route 310 for about 10.5 miles (16.8 kilometers) to the Canadian border. En route, particularly within a mile or two of the customs station, remain alert for owls.

Mississippi

HARRISON EXPERIMENTAL FOREST (near Gulfport)

Owls Present: Barred.
Description: Open pine woodland. An area within the forest known locally as The Hammock should be checked for breeding Barred Owls.
Access: From Gulfport drive north on U. S. Route 49 for about 20 miles (32 kilometers) to the junction with State Route 55.

Turn right on Route 55 and continue another 4.0 miles (6.4 kilometers) to the forest entrance. Enter, drive to the nearby headquarters, and seek additional directions to The Hammock.

NOXUBEE NATIONAL WILDLIFE REFUGE
(near Starkville)

Owls Present: Barred.
Description: A 46,000-acre refuge in which Barred Owls occur mainly in bottomland hardwood and cypress forests.
Access: From Starkville drive south for 17.0 miles (27.2 kilometers) to Mississippi State University and follow refuge signs along Oktoc Road to the refuge.

Missouri
BUSCH MEMORIAL WILDLIFE AREA
(near St. Louis)

Owls Present: Eastern Screech, Great Horned, Barred, Long-eared, and Short-eared.
Description: A 7,000-acre natural area with woodland, open fields, cropland, steep hillsides, streams, and 32 lakes of various sizes. Best owl watching/listening is enjoyed from November through May.
Access: From St. Louis drive west on U. S. Route 61 to the junction with State Route 94, then continue west on State Route 94 for about 0.5 miles (0.8 kilometers) to the wildlife area entrance on the left. The area is open between 6 a.m. and 10 p.m.

CREVE COEUR LAKE (near St. Louis)

Owls Present: Great Horned and Barred.
Description: A park, and road, beside the lake shoreline. Owls occur in the general area and provide birders with opportunities to see them occasionally.
Access: From Interstate 270 on the west side of St. Louis, drive west on Dorsett Road and continue to its end. Turn right and continue downhill to the lake. There turn left and continue to the last parking area. Park, then walk along the trail along the shore of the lake checking trees for owls. Alternatively drive along the road along the edge of the lake in the opposite direction. Check large trees on the right.

LAKE JACOMO COUNTY PARK
(near Kansas City)

Owls Present: Great Horned and Long-eared.
Description: Conifers ringing the lake. Owls sometimes are discovered in winter, in these trees, if careful searches are made.
Access: At the junction of Interstate Routes 435 and 70, near Kansas City, drive east on Interstate 70 for 7.2 miles (11.5 kilometers) to State Route 291. Turn south onto State Route 291 and continue for 4 miles (6.4 kilometers) to Woods Chapel Road. Turn onto that road and continue another 2 miles (3.2 kilometers) to the park entrance.

REED MEMORIAL WILDLIFE AREA
(near Kansas City)

Owls Present: Eastern Screech, Great Horned, Barred, Long-eared, and Short-eared.
Description: A 2,000 acre area with open fields, cropland, woodland, and nine lakes of various sizes. The best owl watching period is from December through April.
Access: From Kansas City, drive east on U. S. Route 50 to the junction with County Route RA at the east edge of Lee's Summit. Turn south onto County Route RA and continue 1.0 mile (1.6 kilometers) to the wildlife area entrance on the left. The area is open between 6 a.m. and 9 p.m.

SCHELL-OSAGE WILDLIFE MANAGEMENT AREA (near Schell City)

Owls Present: Eastern Screech, Great Horned, Barred, Short-eared, and Northern Saw-whet.
Description: A waterfowl hunting area with woodland, lakes, and ponds. Winter and spring are best for owl finding.
Access: From Schell City drive south on Highway AA for 0.5 mile (0.8 kilometer) then turn east onto Highway RA and continue for 3.0 miles (4.8 kilometers) to the headquarters on the left where additional information can be obtained on the status of owls in the area and the best spots for possible owl watching or listening.

SHANKS WILDLIFE AREA (near Ashburn)

Owls Present: Eastern Screech, Great Horned, Barred, and Short-eared.

Description: More than 9,000 acres of Missouri River bottomland forests, marshes, and timbered hills. Winter provides the best owl finding opportunities.

Access: Via Route TT from Route 79, 18 miles (28.8 kilometers) south of Hannibal or 16 miles (25.6 kilometers) north of Louisiana, Missouri.

SQUAW CREEK NATIONAL WILDLIFE REFUGE (near Mound City)

Owls Present: Common Barn, Eastern Screech, Great Horned, Barred, Long-eared, Short-eared, and Northern Saw-whet.

Description: Missouri River bottomlands, 6,900 acres, with marsh, open water, and woodland. Winter provides the best period for owl finding.

Access: From St. Joseph, drive north on Interstate 29 for about 30 miles (48 kilometers) to Exit 79, then continue west on Route 159 for 1.5 miles (2.4 kilometers) to the refuge headquarters on the left. Inquire there for the current status of owls and the best locations where owl finding might be possible.

ST. CHARLES COUNTY AIRPORT
(near St. Charles)

Owls Present: Short-eared.

Description: Grassy areas bordering the airport runways provide Short-eared Owls suitable habitat during winter.

Access: From St. Charles drive north on State Route 94 ignoring the sign 2 miles (3.2 kilometers) outside the city pointing to the airport. Instead, continue about 7.0 miles (11.2 kilometers), then turn left onto Grafton Ferry Road. The airport terminal is a mile beyond on the right. Pass the terminal and take the first road to the right. Then turn right into the parking lot of the large blue Globe Aviation building. From there check for owls on the grassy areas bordering the runways. Do not walk on the runways without permission.

TABERVILLE PRAIRIE (near Appleton City)

Owls Present: Short-eared.

Description: A 1,360-acre area of native prairie and 320 acres of old fields in which Short-eared Owls sometimes appear from December through February.

Access: From Appleton City, in southwestern Missouri, drive east on Route 52 for 1.5 miles (2.4 kilometers), then turn south onto Highway A and continue another 2.0 miles (3.2 kilometers) to Highway H. Turn onto Highway H and continue south for 7.0 miles (11.2 kilometers) to the prairie.

Montana

GLACIER NATIONAL PARK (near West Glacier)

Owls Present: Snowy and Great Gray.

Description: Areas above St. Mary Lake frequently produce Great Gray Owls from July through August. The birds respond quickly to imitations of their calls and sometimes can be called within viewing distance. In winter, Snowy Owls sometimes appear along the shores of Lake McDonald and McDonald Creek where formal Bald Eagle viewing opportunities are available. Park rangers can provide full details.

Access: From West Glacier, on U. S. Route 2, drive north into the park. Stop at the headquarters or information center for a map and other details about owls in the park including Great Gray Owls in the St. Mary Lake area.

Nebraska

NORTH PLATTE AREA

Owls Present: Burrowing.

Description: Rolling, treeless sandhills in which Burrowing Owls sometimes are seen from the highway.

Access: From North Platte, drive north on U. S. Route 83 for about 28 miles (44.8 kilometers) remaining alert during the last 20 miles (32 kilometers) for Burrowing Owls adjacent to the road.

PIONEERS PARK (in Lincoln)

Owls Present: Long-eared.

Description: A 600-acre park with many pine plantings in which Long-eared Owls frequently are found in winter.

Access: From U. S. Route 77/State Route 2, turn west onto South Street and continue to Park Boulevard. There, at Gooch Mill, turn left onto Park Boulevard and continue to West Van Dorn Street. Turn right onto Van Dorn Street, pass the entrance to Wilderness Park, and continue for 1.5 miles (2.4 kilometers) to Coddington Avenue. Turn south onto Coddington Avenue and drive 0.2 mile (0.3 kilometer) to the entrance to Pioneers Park on the right. Enter, park in a suitable place, then search on foot for owls in pine or other conifer plantings.

New Jersey
CAPE MAY POINT

Owls Present: Common Barn, Eastern Screech, Great Horned, Long-eared, and Northern Saw-whet.
Description: Woodlots, marshes, open areas, and beaches in the vicinity of the lighthouse in Cape May Point State Park. Common Barn Owls sometimes can be seen at night flying in the vicinity of the lighthouse, and owl trapping and banding programs are conducted at the point (contact the park office for details). September to late November or early December provide the best owl finding opportunities.
Access: Follow the Garden State Parkway south into the town of Cape May, then continue after leaving the Parkway to Cape May Point a few miles farther south. Well marked signs point the way. In the vicinity of the Point, head toward the lighthouse and park beside it or in parking areas within the state park. From there explore the area for owls and other birdlife.

GREAT SWAMP NATIONAL WILDLIFE REFUGE (near Basking Ridge)

Owls Present: Eastern Screech, Great Horned, and Barred.
Description: A 5,800-acre refuge in which a boardwalk allows visitors to walk into the interior of the swamp. Owls can be heard on spring evenings.
Access: The refuge headquarters is located on Pleasant Plains Road near Basking Ridge, and the observation area and boardwalk is located on the New Vernon-Long Hill Road. Refuge signs direct visitors to each area from various intersections in the vicinity of the refuge.

MANAHAWKIN FISH AND WILDLIFE AREA
(near Manahawkin)

Owls Present: Short-eared.

Description: A salt marsh, with diked ponds and an access road, over which Short-eared Owls sometimes occur during winter at dusk.

Access: From the junction of Exit 63 of the Garden State Parkway and State Route 72 near Manahawkin, drive east on State Route 72 toward Long Beach Island. At the junction of State Route 72 and U. S. Route 9, turn north onto U. S. Route 9 and continue a short distance to a traffic light at Route 9 and 180 in Manahawkin. Continue past the light for a short distance to the first right turn after the light. Turn right onto this road and follow it past woodland to salt marsh and diked ponds. Park at a suitable spot along the road, or walk as far as possible along the unpaved road extending into the marsh and use a small bridge over a tidal creek as an elevated observation post to scan the marsh for birds.

New Mexico

BIGNAL PEAK (near Silver City)

Owls Present: Flammulated.

Description: A 9,000-foot-high peak with patches of aspen in which Flammulated Owls nest. The birds sometimes can be "squeaked up" at entrance holes in trees.

Access: Follow the directions to Cherry Creek Canyon, then continue 3 miles (4.8 kilometers) farther on State Route 25 to Forest Road 154 on the right. Turn right onto Forest Road 154 and carefully follow this rough road for about 2 miles (3.2 kilometers) upward to aspen patches where owls may be encountered.

BITTER LAKE NATIONAL WILDLIFE REFUGE (near Roswell)

Owls Present: Burrowing.

Description: A prairie dog colony, near the refuge entrance, in which Burrowing Owls occur.

Access: From Roswell drive north on U.S. Routes 70 and 285 (Main Street) and continue for 0.5 mile (0.8 kilometer) past the Berrendo Bridge. Then turn right at a refuge directional sign and continue for about 12 miles (19.2 kilometers) to the refuge. Just before entering the refuge check the prairie dog colony on the right for owls.

CHERRY CREEK CANYON (near Silver City)

Owls Present: Flammulated, Northern Pygmy, and Spotted.
Description: A wooded canyon in the Pinos Altos Mountains in which owls nest and otherwise occur on the sides of the canyon. Northern Pygmy Owls sometimes call during the day and sound somewhat like chipmunks.
Access: From the junction of U. S. Route 180 and State Route 25, drive north on State Route 25 for about 8 miles (12.8 kilometers) to Pinos Altos, then continue somewhat farther along State Route 25 to Cherry Creek Canyon which can be searched for owls.

GAGE AREA (near Deming)

Owls Present: Common Barn, Great Horned, Burrowing, and Short-eared.
Description: An unpaved road leading across desert-grass-land. Owls sometimes are seen along the road at night during autumn and winter.
Access: From Deming, in southwestern New Mexico, drive west on Interstate 10 for about 33 miles (52.8 kilometers) to the hamlet of Gage located north of I-10. There follow an unpaved road north for about 10 miles (16 kilometers) toward Whitewater, to a locked gate, then return again to Gage on the same road while remaining alert for owls along the way.

GLENWOOD AREA

Owls Present: Northern Pygmy (occasional) and Elf.
Description: Scattered trees and groves of cottonwoods in and around Glenwood. Owls call at night in such habitats near motels.
Access: From Silver City, drive northwest on U.S. Route 180 for about 63 miles (100.8 kilometers) to Glenwood. There check suitable habitat at night and listen for Elf Owls and an occasional Northern Pygmy Owl.

New York

AVON AREA

Owls Present: Short-eared.
Description: Fields, trees, and other perches along Nations Road along which concentrations of Short-eared Owls occur from December through March as they hunt over fields or perch on trees or other elevated objects. A particularly good roosting tree is located at the intersection of Nations and Hogmire Roads.
Access: From Exit 46 of Interstate 90 (New York State Thruway) near Avon, follow New York Route 15 south for some 10 miles (16 kilometers) to the intersection of New York Routes 5 and 20. Turn west (right) onto New York Route 20, continue to the traffic circle in Avon, then drive another 0.2 miles (0.3 kilometers) west to New York Route 39. Turn south (left) onto Route 39, continue 1.7 miles (2.7 kilometers) to Fowlerville Road, turn right and continue westward 2.4 miles (3.8 kilometers) to Nations Road. Turn left onto Nations Road and search for owls along its length to the intersection with Hogmire Road and the owl roosting tree.

BRADDOCK BAY STATE PARK (near Rochester)

Owls Present: Snowy, Long-eared, Short-eared, and Northern Saw-whet.
Description: A well known park (and major spring hawk lookout) with marshes in which Snowy Owls occur during winter and Short-eared Owls occur in spring, and pine woods in which Long-eared and Northern Saw-whet Owls occur from late March to late April.
Access: On the north side of Rochester, follow the Lake Ontario State Parkway west for a few miles to the East Manitou Road exit. Leave the parkway, turn right at the stop sign, then drive about 500 feet (150 meters) to the Braddock Bay State Park entrance. Enter the park, drive within view of marshes or woods and check for owls.

BUFFALO WATERFRONT

Owls Present: Snowy.
Description: Breakwalls along two miles of lake front between the Erie Basin Marina (near downtown Buffalo) and the

diked impoundments at South Buffalo. Snowy Owls may appear between late October and early April.

Access: From the junction of Interstate 190 (New York Thruway) and State Route 5 South (the Buffalo Skyway), turn onto Route 5 South. Cross the high-level Skyway bridge and leave that highway at the first Fuhrmann Boulevard ramp. Then follow signs for the Coast Guard in order to arrive at the Times Beach impoundment which is immediately adjacent (south of) the Coast Guard property at the end of Fuhrmann Boulevard. Dikes and breakwalls, from this point south along Fuhrmann Boulevard for the next 2.5 miles (4 kilometers) provide good owl watching opportunities. Another good owl finding site is reached from the Skyway (see above) and continuing to downtown Buffalo. Then exit and follow Marine Drive behind apartments to the Erie Basin Marina (opposite the mouth of the Buffalo River from the Coast Guard). Look for owls in this area, too.

CANNONSVILLE RESERVOIR AREA
(near Deposit)

Owls Present: Great Horned, Snowy.

Description: A reservoir dam and surrounding areas in which Snowy (and Great Horned) Owls sometimes occur during winter.

Access: From the junction of New York Routes 17 and 10 near Deposit, drive northwest on Route 10 for 3 miles (4.8 kilometers) to the reservoir. Check all roads and surrounding areas in the area for owls.

COXSACKIE AREA

Owls Present: Common Barn, Eastern Screech, Great Horned, Snowy, Short-eared, and Northern Saw-whet.

Description: Fields and isolated cedar trees southwest of Coxsackie along U. S. Route 9 for some 3–6 miles (4.8–9.6 kilometers) from town. Other roads in the area also may produce owls and other raptors. Winter is the best time for observing these birds in this area.

Access: From Coxsackie, get onto U.S. Route 9 and check for owls in fields and in cedar trees along the road.

ELK LAKE (near Lake Placid)

Owls Present: Great Horned and Barred.
Description: A lake set amid coniferous and hardwood forests.
Access: Near North Hudson follow Exit 29 off Interstate 87 and continue west for 5.0 miles (8 kilometers) on Blue Ridge Road. At the end of the road turn right and continue to the lake and Elk Lake lodge. A foot trail runs from the lodge to the top of Mt. Marcy.

FOREST LAWN CEMETERY (in Buffalo)

Owls Present: Eastern Screech, Great Horned, Long-eared, and Northern Saw-whet.
Description: Dense vegetation at the end of the cemetery in which owls sometimes roost in winter.
Access: Follow Delaware Avenue (State Route 384) for about 2.0 miles (3.2 kilometers) from center city Buffalo to the cemetery.

GILGO BEACH (on Long Island)

Owls Present: Snowy, and Short-eared.
Description: A barrier beach island with dunes on the south shore and marshes on the north shore. Snowy and Short-eared Owls sometimes are reported in winter.
Access: From Babylon drive east on State Route 27 or 27A, then south on the Robert Moses Causeway to Captree State Park. At the park drive west on Ocean Parkway to Gilgo Beach, just west of Gilgo State Park, and park in the village parking lot. Walk east from there to a former Coast Guard station. Check for owls in its vicinity as well as elsewhere in the Gilgo Beach area.

GRAND ISLAND (near Buffalo)

Owls Present: Short-eared (up to 30 per day).
Description: Fields along the north side of Ransom Road. Owls use the area from mid-December to late February.
Access: From Buffalo drive north on Interstate 190, cross the South Grand Island Bridge, then take the first exit north of the bridge (Beaver Island State Park). Drive east on Staley Road for 0.25 mile (0.4 kilometer), turn left onto Stony Point Road

and follow it for 2.0 miles (3.2 kilometers) to Ransom Road. Turn right onto Ransom Road and drive for 0.75 mile (1.2 kilometers) to International Lane. Turn left onto International Lane and, following it, check for owls hunting over the fields north of Ransom Road—but best seen from International Lane.

HEART LAKE (near Lake Placid)

Owls Present: Great Horned and Barred.
Description: Adirondack forest in which owls sometimes are heard near the lodge, or campsites, at the lake.
Access: From Lake Placid drive south on State Route 73 to Elba, turn right, and continue another 5.0 miles (8.0 kilometers) to the Adirondack Lodge at Heart Lake.

JAMAICA BAY WILDLIFE REFUGE (in New York City)

Owls Present: Short-eared.
Description: Ponds with dikes, marsh, mud flats, and other habitats over which Short-eared Owls hunt during winter.
Access: From J.F. Kennedy Airport, in Queens, drive west on State Route 27 for about 2 miles (3.2 kilometers) to its junction with Cross Bay Boulevard. Turn south onto Cross Bay Boulevard and continue for 1.4 miles (2.2 kilometers) to an obvious sign for the refuge entrance. Secure an entry permit at the park's interpretive building before entering the refuge. West Pond is particularly good Short-eared Owl habitat in winter.

JONES BEACH STATE PARK (on Long Island)

Owls Present: Common Barn, Long-eared, and Northern Saw-whet; in winter, Snowy and Short-eared.
Description: A 2,413-acre park on a barrier beach island.
Access: From the Long Island Expressway or the Southern State Parkway drive south on the Meadowbrook State Parkway into Jones Beach State Park. Park in West End Parking Field 2, then walk westward to a jetty at Jones Inlet. En route look for owls (Common Barn, Long-eared, and Northern Saw-whet) in pines east of the West End Parking Field 1. In winter, Snowy and Short-eared Owls may occur on the dunes.

MONTAUK POINT AREA (on Long Island)

Owls Present: Snowy and Short-eared.
Description: The eastern end of Long Island with various dunes, ponds, marshes, and other habitats in which owls may appear during some winters.
Access: From New York City drive east on State Route 27 for the entire length of Long Island to the Montauk Point Area where owl watchers should check wetlands, dunes, and other likely areas for owls.

NIAGARA FALLS AIRPORT

Owls Present: Snowy.
Description: Fields, poles, and tops of buildings immediately behind the airport complex and eastward along Walmore Avenue bordering Bell Aerospace. Look for Snowy Owls in winter.
Access: From the junction of Interstate 190 and U. S. Route 62 in Niagara Falls, drive east on Route 62 (Pine Avenue) for about 2 miles (3.2 kilometers) to Niagara Falls Boulevard in front of the Niagara Falls International Airport. Continue east on Niagara Falls Boulevard past the front of the airport, pass Bell Aerospace factory, then take the first road left (Walmore Road). Follow Walmore Road for about 1.5 miles (2.4 kilometers) to its end. Turn left onto Lockport Road which passes along the rear of the airport. Look for owls along the length of Walmore Road and at least 1.5 miles (2.4 kilometers) along Lockport Road.

ORIENT BEACH STATE PARK (on Long Island)

Owls Present: Snowy and Short-eared.
Description: A 357-acre park with beaches and meadows at the northeastern end of Long Island. Owls occasionally appear in winter—Short-eared over meadows and Snowy Owls on beaches.
Access: From Greenport drive east on State Route 25 to Narrow River Road, about 2.0 miles (3.2 kilometers) west of Orient Point, then continue south on Narrow River Road to Orient Beach State Park. Park in the parking areas provided and explore the area on foot looking for owls.

PERCH RIVER MARSH (near Watertown)

Owls Present: Snowy.

Description: A 3,000-acre marsh formed by a dam. Snowy Owls sometimes hunt below the dam in winter.

Access: From Watertown drive north on State Route 12 for 7.0 miles (11.2 kilometers) to Parish Road. Turn right onto Parish Road, continue another 0.75 mile (1.2 kilometers), then turn left into a parking lot. Park and explore the area on foot.

REED ROAD SWAMP (near Rochester)

Owls Present: Great Horned, Barred, and Northern Saw-whet.

Description: A moist deciduous woodland in which heavy understory vegetation grows. A highway passes through the swamp, and a foot path leads into remote sections of the swamp from Reed Road.

Access: From Rochester follow State Route 383 south to Ballantyne Road, turn right onto Ballantyne Road and drive to Reed Road. There turn left and continue on Reed Road for about 0.5 mile (0.8 kilometer) down a hill to the swamp. The path leading into the swamp begins from the west side of Reed Road.

STEWART PARK (near Ithaca)

Owls Present: Great Horned.

Description: A partially wooded park with dense understory vegetation at the southern end of Cayuga Lake. Great Horned Owls occasionally nest not far from the path.

Access: From Ithaca drive north on State Route 13 for a short distance, then follow the signs to the park.

North Carolina

BLUE RIDGE PARKWAY (near Waynesville)

Owls Present: Northern Saw-whet.

Description: A series of calling and/or listening stations using roadside overlooks along the Blue Ridge Parkway, in the southern portion of the Great Balsam Mountains and Pisgah Ridge. Island-like areas with extensive spruce-fir forests are especially productive for finding Northern Saw-whet Owls. Best seasons are from early April to mid-June at night between midnight and dawn.

Access: From Waynesville drive south on U. S. Routes 19 and 23 to the entrance to the Blue Ridge Parkway. Enter the parkway, drive northeast, and stop at the various sites mentioned below to listen for, or attempt to call up, Northern Saw-whet Owls. More than 10 sites are reported along this section of the parkway between Lone Bald Overlook and Fork River Bald. The following are particularly productive.

1. Spruce Ridge—Check the area just east of Lone Bald Overlook.

2. Richland Balsam—Check from a spot along the parkway about 0.4 mile (0.6 kilometer) east of Lone Bald Overlook.

3. Richland Balsam—Explore the nature trail leading from the Jackson-Haywood Overlook as it follows the south side of Richland Balsam (mile 431.4) to its peak. Listen for, or call up, owls en route especially within the first 250 yards of the trail entrance.

4. Chestnut Ridge—From the Cowee Mountain Overlook, listen for owls on the south slope of Richland Balsam below the overlook.

5. Big Beartrail Ridge—From a spot some 100 feet northeast of the parkway road through Big Beartrail Ridge listen for owls.

6. Beartrap Gap—From the Beartrap Gap Overlook listen for owls on an unnamed peak northwest of the overlook.

7. Haywood Gap—The area near Sweetwater Spring, just below the point where the parkway cuts through Haywood Gap, sometimes produces birds on the north slope of Parker Knob.

8. Tanasee Bald—From the Tanasee Bald Overlook listen for owls on the slope of the peak about 100 yards southwest of the overlook.

9. Devil's Courthouse—The north slope of the peak adjacent to the trail leading from the parkway sometimes produces birds.

10. Silvermine Bald—From a spot about 0.2 mile (0.3 kilometer) west of Shuck Ridge, owls sometimes are heard calling from the south slope of the bald above the parkway.

MOUNT MITCHELL (near Asheville)

Owls Present: Northern Saw-whet.

Description: A 6,684-foot-high mountain along the Blue Ridge Parkway. Listen for Northern Saw-whet Owls at night from the parking area near the mountain's summit.

Access: From Asheville drive east on State Route 694 to the Blue Ridge Parkway, then continue northeast on the Parkway to State Route 128 near Mt. Mitchell. Turn left onto State Route 128 and follow it for 4.5 miles (7.2 kilometers) to the parking area near the summit of the mountain. Owl watchers wishing to remain at the parking area after 8 p.m., at which time the road leading up Mt. Mitchell is closed for the night, must arrange with park officials to be left out after the road is closed, or camp overnight in a campground close to the parking area.

North Dakota
BELFIELD AREA

Owls Present: Burrowing.

Description: Rolling prairie on which Burrowing Owls sometimes are seen.

Access: From Belfield, drive on U. S. Route 85 either north or south of town for various distances remaining alert for owls near the highway.

MEDINA TO STEELE AREA

Owls Present: Burrowing.

Description: A section of Interstate 94 along which Burrowing Owls occur in scattered groups.

Access: From Medina, drive west on Interstate 94 to Steele. Remain alert for groups of owls near the highway, and also watch for various diurnal raptors including Ferruginous Hawks.

Ohio
AULLWOOD AUDUBON CENTER
(near Dayton)

Owls Present: Great Horned.

Description: A 70-acre refuge with mixed habitat. Great Horned Owls nest on the refuge.

Access: From Dayton drive north on Interstate 75 to the junction with Interstate 70. Follow Interstate 70 west to its junction with State Route 48. Turn onto State Route 48 and drive north for a short distance to U. S. Route 40. Turn right (east) and follow U. S. Route 40 across a large dam. The entrance to the Aullwood Audubon Center is on the right at the end of the guard rail for the dam. Ask at the headquarters building for the best owl watching/listening spots.

BEAVER CREEK STATE WILDLIFE AREA
(near Bryan)

Owls Present: Barred.

Description: A 153-acre site with forest, fields, brushy areas, and a creek.

Access: From Bryan drive north on State Route 15 for 6 miles (9.6 kilometers) to the site in Williams County.

BURKE LAKEFRONT AIRPORT (in Cleveland)

Owls Present: Snowy.

Description: Fields in a small downtown airport. Look for Snowy Owls during the winter.

Access: At the junction of State Route 2 and East Ninth Street in Cleveland drive north on North Marginal Drive to the airport. Follow the road eastward along the fence around the airport looking for owls in the area inside the fence.

CALIFORNIA NATURE PRESERVE
(in Cincinnati)

Owls Present: Great Horned.

Description: A 60-acre wooded area through which a small creek flows. Listen for Great Horned Owls in the area.

Access: From Cincinnati drive east on U.S. Route 52 to the preserve entrance about 1 mile (1.6 kilometers) past a bridge over the Little Miami River.

CINCINNATI NATURE CENTER
(near Cincinnati)

Owls Present: Eastern Screech, Great Horned, and Barred.

Description: A 750-acre nature reserve containing hardwood forest, fields, and a lake and ponds. A nature center building serves as headquarters.
Access: From the junction of Interstate 275 and State Route 32, drive east on State Route 32 to Gleneste-Williamsville Road, turn left and continue to a "T." Turn right and drive about two blocks, then turn left onto Tealtown Road. Continue ahead for about 2 miles (3.2 kilometers) to the nature center entrance on the left.

CRANE CREEK STATE PARK (near Oak Harbor)

Owls Present: Eastern Screech, Great Horned, Northern Saw-whet.
Description: A 2,600-acre area with Lake Erie beach, ponds, marshes, fields, and woodland. A nature center operates in the park. Eastern Screech Owls and Great Horned Owls are permanent residents, whereas Northern Saw-whet Owls use cedar trees and grapevine thickets during late March and April.
Access: On State Route 2, 17 miles (27.2 kilometers) west of Port Clinton, enter the park. Seek the latest bird finding information at the nature center.

ENGLEWOOD RESERVE (near Dayton)

Owls Present: Long-eared and Northern Saw-whet.
Description: A pine planting in a 1,000-acre section of the Stillwater River valley.
Access: Follow the directions to the Aullwood Audubon Center (given earlier) but turn left at the end of the dam's guard rail and go into the reserve.

FORT HILL STATE MEMORIAL (near Hillsboro)

Owls Present: Great Horned and Barred.
Description: A 1,197-acre park containing diverse habitats and a prehistoric Indian enclosure.
Access: From Hillsboro drive southeast on State Route 124 for 16 miles (25.6 kilometers) to the junction with State Route 41. Turn north onto State Route 41 and continue 3 miles (4.8 kilometers) to the park entrance on the left.

GREENLAWN CEMETERY (in Columbus)

Owls Present: Long-eared and Northern Saw-whet.
Description: A mixed habitat of open areas and trees. In March and April owls roost in conifers in the cemetery.
Access: From the center of Columbus drive west on Interstate 71 to the Greenlawn Avenue (west) exit. Leave Interstate 71 at that exit and follow Greenlawn Avenue west directly to the cemetery.

HAMBDEN ORCHARD WILDLIFE AREA (near Hambden)

Owls Present: Eastern Screech, Barred.
Description: An 841-acre site with woodland, pools, fields, and an old orchard.
Access: From Hambden, drive south on State Route 608 for 3 miles (4.8 kilometers) to the site.

HIGHBANKS METROPOLITAN PARK (near Columbus)

Owls Present: Eastern Screech, Great Horned, and Barred.
Description: A 1,050-acre upland forest with deep ravines.
Access: From the junction of Interstate 270 and U. S. Route 23, drive north on U.S. Route 23 for about 2 miles (3.2 kilometers) to the park.

KILLDEER PLAINS WILDLIFE AREA (near Marion)

Owls Present: Snowy, Short-eared.
Description: Some 8,000 acres of wetlands, woodland, fields, and cropland. Snowy Owls appear only rarely during winter, but Short-eared Owls frequently hunt over fields west and south of the headquarters building.
Access: At the junction of U.S. Route 23 and State Route 294, some 14 miles (22.4 kilometers) northwest of Marion, turn east and follow State Route 294 through Harpster to County Road 115. There drive south on County Road 115 for about 1 mile (1.6 kilometers) to the site.

MIAMI-WHITEWATER FOREST COUNTY PARK (near Cincinnati)

Owls Present: Great Horned.
Description: A 2,031-acre forested area in which several lakes also are located. Great Horned Owls nest in the park.
Access: From Cincinnati drive west on Interstate 74 to Dry Forks Road, then continue north for about 2 miles (3.2 kilometers) on Dry Forks Road to the park entrance.

MILL CREEK PARK (in Youngstown)

Owls Present: Eastern Screech and Barred.
Description: A 2,389-acre park noted for its cliffs, ravines, gorge, and fine woodland. Eastern Screech and Barred Owls nest in the park.
Access: Three entrances to the park are available—along U.S. Route 62 (Canfield Road), at Falls and Glenwood Avenues, and at the Mahoning Avenue Bridge.

Oklahoma
BUFFALO AREA

Owls Present: Burrowing.
Description: A section of U.S. Route 64 extending westward from Buffalo across the rolling prairie. Burrowing Owls sometimes are seen near the road in this area.
Access: From Buffalo, drive west on U.S. Route 64 for about 6 miles (9.6 kilometers) looking for owls along the way.

GUYMON AREA

Owls Present: Common Barn and Burrowing.
Description: A section of U.S. Route 64 along which Burrowing Owls occur in prairie dog towns, and Common Barn Owls may occur in deserted buildings.
Access: From Guymon, drive north and west on U.S. Route 64 checking likely owl habitats along the way.

JAYBUCKLE SPRING (near Reed)

Owls Present: Burrowing.

Description: Prairie dog towns, near the spring, in which Burrowing Owls sometimes are seen.

Access: From Mangum, drive west on State Route 9 for 11 miles (17.6 kilometers) to Reed, then turn north onto another road and continue for 4 miles (6.4 kilometers) to Jaybuckle Spring.

Oregon
FORT KLAMATH AREA

Owls Present: Great Gray.

Description: The edge of a meadow bordered with coniferous forest. Look for Great Gray Owls at dusk when the birds emerge from the forest to hunt prey over the meadow.

Access: From Klamath Agency, drive north on State Route 232 for about 6 miles (9.6 kilometers) to the junction with State Route 62. There turn northwestward onto State Route 62 and continue for 1 mile (1.6 kilometers) to Fort Klamath. Search carefully along Route 62 between State Route 232 and the town for owls.

FORT ROCK STATE MONUMENT (near Bend)

Owls Present: Great Horned.

Description: A 300-foot-high volcanic cone in whose clefts owls and other birds of prey nest.

Access: From Bend go south on U. S. Route 97 for 4 miles (6.4 kilometers) to the junction with Forest Service Road 1821. Then turn southward onto Forest Service Road 1821 and continue for about 50 miles (80 kilometers) to Fort Rock which rises high above the surrounding flats.

SAUVIE ISLAND WILDLIFE MANAGEMENT AREA (near Portland)

Owls Present: Great Horned, Short-eared, and Northern Saw-whet.

Description: A 13,000-acre wildlife area separated into three units with sloughs, lakes, and forested bottomlands. In winter, owls, especially Short-eared Owls, sometimes can be found.

Access: From Portland, drive west onto U.S. Route 30 from its junction with Interstate 5, cross the St. Johns Bridge, and continue 3.5 miles (5.6 kilometers) past the bridge to the

Sauvie Island Bridge (well marked). Turn right, cross the birdge, and turn left onto Sauvie Island Road. Continue 2.5 miles (4 kilometers) to Reeder Road. Turn right onto Reeder Road and drive 1.2 miles (1.9 kilometer) to Oak Island Road. There turn left onto Oak Island Road and continue another 3 miles (4.8 kilometers) to the wildlife area.

SOUTH BEACH STATE PARK (near Newport)

Owls Present: Snowy.
Description: A protected section of the Oregon coastline along which Snowy Owls sometimes appear in winter.
Access: From Newport drive south on U.S. Route 101 for a few miles to the park turnoff.

WRIGHT'S POINT (near Burns)

Owls Present: Burrowing.
Description: A plateau covered with sagebrush. Burrowing Owls sometimes perch on utility poles along the road.
Access: From Burns, go east on U.S. Route 20 for 2 miles (3.2 kilometers) then turn south onto State Route 205 and continue for approximately 8 miles (12.8 kilometers) to Wright's Point. Continue on, looking for owls, where the road goes down to alkaline flats.

Pennsylvania

BELTZVILLE LAKE AREA (near Lehighton)

Owls Present: Short-eared.
Description: Open fields with scattered trees adjacent to a large lake. In late autumn and winter Short-eared Owls sometimes hunt over these fields late in the day, and some roost in suitable trees.
Access: From Lehighton, drive northeast on U.S. Route 209 for about 3 miles (4.8 kilometers). Just beyond the Pennsylvania Turnpike entrance, at a Beltzville Lake sign, turn left. Cross a small bridge, continue several hundred feet into a tiny village and, at another sign for the lake, turn sharply right onto another road and continue for several miles past the Beltzville lake dam. Somewhat farther along this road look for various access roads leading into open fields, boat landing areas, and recreation areas. Check these areas for owls.

CAMP HORSESHOE (near Orefield)

Owls Present: Eastern Screech, Great Horned, and Long-eared.
Description: A hillside conifer forest, bisected by a stream and a road, adjacent to old fields and other agricultural areas.
Access: From the junction of U.S. Routes 22 and 309, just west of Allentown, drive north on U.S. Route 309 for a few miles to a blinker light in the village of Orefield. Turn left at the blinker and drive about 1.1 miles (1.7 kilometers) to a road leading off toward the right. Turn right onto that road and continue to a covered bridge. Just before entering the birdge turn left onto an unpaved road and follow it past Camp Horseshoe on the right to a hillside covered with dense conifers. Listen in this area for owls. Winter and spring are best for night owl prowling in the area.

FOGELSVILLE POND (near Allentown)

Owls Present: Eastern Screech and Great Horned.
Description: A small pond and dam bordered on one side by a forested hillside and the other side by a road, woodland, and agricultural fields.
Access: From the junction of U.S. Route 22 and State Route 100, west of Allentown, drive north on State Route 100 for 1.2 miles (1.9 kilometers) to a turnoff road to the right marked for Penn State University. Turn right and continue straight ahead a short distance to a stop sign at a cross roads. Turn left there and drive another short distance to a wide shoulder of the road on the left. Pull onto the shoulder and listen for Eastern Screech Owls on the forested hillside on the far side of the pond on your right.

KLINE'S RUN PARK (near Wrightsville)

Owls Present: Common Barn, Great Horned, and Long-eared.
Description: Pine plantings on a hillside overlooking the nearby Susquehanna River. Owls sometimes roost in the trees.
Access: From the junction of State Routes 462 and 624 in Wrightsville, drive south on State Route 624 (Front Street in Wrightsville) for 3.5 miles (5.6 kilometers) to the Kline's Run Park entrance. Turn right into the park, then climb the

nearby hillside on foot and look carefully among the pines for roosting owls from autumn through spring.

LEASER LAKE (near New Tripoli)

Owls Present: Eastern Screech and Great Horned.

Description: An artificial lake of considerable size surrounded by mixed coniferous-deciduous woodland, upland fields, and a parking lot. The best owl watching is done at night adjacent to the woodland along the northern sides of the lake.

Access: From the junction of State Routes 143 and 309 at New Tripoli, drive south on State Route 143 for 4.9 miles (7.8 kilometers) to the road leading to Leaser Lake on the right. Turn right onto that road and continue ahead for another 0.6 mile (0.9 kilometer) to a "T" at which point turn left and drive 0.5 mile (0.8 kilometer) to the parking lot on the left. Park in the lot, then check the adjacent woodland along the northern side of the lake for owls.

LEWIS STATE PARK (near Wrightsville)

Owls Present: Great Horned and Long-eared.

Description: A small pine planting on a hillside. Owls use the trees as roost sites from autumn through spring.

Access: From the junction of State Routes 462 and 624 in Wrightsville, drive west on State Route 462 (Old Route 30) for 0.8 mile (1.2 kilometers) to Cool Creek Road adjacent to a golf course. Turn left (south) onto Cool Creek Road and drive 1.4 miles (2.2 kilometers) to Pisgah Road on the right. Turn right (west) onto Pisgah Road and continue ahead for 0.5 mile (0.8 kilometer) to the park entrance on the left. Turn into the park, continue a few feet to the parking lot, and park there. Then walk south for a few feet to the pine plantings which should be checked carefully for roosting owls.

MIDDLE CREEK WILDLIFE MANAGEMENT AREA (near Kleinfeltersville)

Owls Present: Common Barn, Eastern Screech, Great Horned, Snowy, Long-eared, Short-eared, and Northern Saw-whet.

Description: A 5,000-acre wildlife area containing a large lake, ponds, creeks, swamp, meadows, pastures, and woodland in which owls live or visit. In winter, during years when rodents are abundant, Short-eared Owls sometimes are reported hunting over portions of the property. There is a visitor center and museum available for public use.

Access: From Kleinfeltersville, Lebanon County, follow the signs south for about 1.0 mile (1.6 kilometers) to the visitor center where literature and information can be secured.

NEW BLOOMFIELD AREA

Owls Present: Common Barn (rare), Eastern Screech, Great Horned, Barred, Long-eared (uncommon), Snowy (rare), and Northern Saw-whet (rare).

Description: Rural countryside in close proximity to secondary and rural roads within a 7.5 mile (12.0 kilometer) radius of New Bloomfield. Eastern Screech and Great Horned Owls are commonly heard and/or seen during winter.

Access: From the town of New Bloomfield explore rural roads in the area making frequent stops to listen for, or call up, owls. Particularly productive owl watching/listening areas are in the vicinity of State Game Land 256, Little Buffalo State Park, and the villages of Falling Spring and Mannsville.

NEW TRIPOLI AREA

Owls Present: Eastern Screech.

Description: A wooded area beside a creek set within an agricultural region. At night Eastern Screech Owls sometimes respond to calls or tapes.

Access: From the junction of State Routes 143 and 309 at New Tripoli, drive south on State Route 143 for 1.4 miles (2.2 kilometers) to a paved road leading to the right. Turn right onto that road and continue another 0.4 mile (0.6 kilometer) to the wooded area and creek adjacent to the highway. Pull off the road and listen or call up owls from there.

NOCKAMIXON STATE PARK
(near Quakertown)

Owls Present: Great Horned, Barred, Long-eared, and Northern Saw-whet.

Description: A large state park in which extensive pine plantations and other woodland provide suitable owl habitat.

Access: From Quakertown drive south on State Route 313 for a few miles to the junction with State Route 563. Turn left onto State Route 563 and continue a few miles to various entrances to the park. Enter and explore various pine plantations on foot after parking in one of the parking lots.

PEACE VALLEY PARK (near Doylestown)

Owls Present: Common Barn, Eastern Screech, Great Horned, Snowy, Long-eared, Short-eared, and Northern Saw-whet.

Description: A 1,500-acre county park containing woodland, fields, wetlands, and a large lake. Owl watching/listening is especially productive on the park's 300-acre nature center, but can be enjoyed as well elsewhere in the park.

Access: From the junction of U.S. Route 611 and State Route 313 near Doylestown, drive west on State Route 313 for 1.4 miles (2.2 kilometers) to a traffic light at Fountainville. Turn left onto Ferry Road and continue 0.7 mile (1.1 kilometers) to Chapman Road and a nature center sign on the right. Turn right onto Chapman Road and continue a short distance, across a bridge, to the nature center on the right. Listen for, or call up, owls in the area of the nature center.

PHILADELPHIA

Owls Present: Great Horned.

Description: Despite its large urban setting, owl watching is possible within Philadelphia at several locations including the following two sites.

    1. Fairmount Park — Woodland (hemlocks and tulip trees) on a hillside in a section of the park in northwestern Philadelphia. Owl finding opportunities occur from January to May. To visit the site drive south from the junction of Interstate 278 (Pennsylvania Turnpike) and U. S. Route 422 near Norristown on U. S. Route 422 (Germantown Pike) to the Philadelphia city line. Then continue ahead into Philadelphia on U. S. Route 422 for about 0.5 mile (0.8 kilometer) to Bells Mill Road. Turn right (west) onto Bells Mill Road and continue to its intersection with Wissahickon Drive. Park in one of two parking lots (lock your car), walk to the intersection at the stop sign, then walk south on the drive for about 100 feet. There follow the bridle path on the right through a

small grove of hemlocks and up a steep hill. Turn left at the top and walk along the cross path to the point where it turns downhill. Look for owls in that area in large tulip trees or lower in large grape vines.

2. Schuylkill Valley Nature Center — A woodland on the nature center's property in which two large white pine trees provide nesting sites for Great Horned Owls almost every year. Best owl watching opportunities are from January to May. To visit the Center follow the above directions to Bells Mill Road. Turn right (west) onto Bells Mill Road and follow it for a considerable distance to Ridge Pike. Cross Ridge Pike and continue on what is now named Spring Lane to Hagy's Mill Road. Turn left onto Hagy's Mill Road and drive a short distance to the entrance road into the nature center on the right. Enter the center's extensive private property and drive to the headquarters building. Pay a small entrance fee there, pick up a map of the Center property, and any available information on the status of owls. Then walk to the best owl sites in woodland along Ravine Loop west of Bluebird Field.

PINE SWAMP AREA (near Kempton)

Owls Present: Eastern Screech, Great Horned, and Barred.
Description: An area of mixed coniferous-deciduous forest, open fields, and a creek through which a narrow rural road extends. Best owl watching/listening is enjoyed during winter and early spring.
Access: From the village of Eckville, at the south base of Hawk Mountain Sanctuary near Kempton, enter the Pine Creek Road near the Appalachian Trail marker and follow it through the Pine Creek area until it rejoins the main road to Kempton. Stop at likely owl habitat to listen for, or call up, owls. Alternatively, from the junction of U.S. Route 22 and State Route 143 near Lenhartsville drive north on State Route 143 for 4.0 miles (6.4 kilometers) to a crossroad. Turn left onto that road (which leads to Hawk Mountain Sanctuary) and continue toward the sanctuary for about 3.2 miles (5.1 kilometers) to the Pine Swamp Road on the left. Turn left onto the road and follow it for 2.3 miles (3.6 kilometers) to its terminus at Eckville and the highway leading to Hawk Mountain.

TYLER ARBORETUM (near Newtown Square)

Owls Present: Eastern Screech, Great Horned, and Northern Saw-whet.

Description: A 700-acre arboretum containing excellent cover for owls and other wildlife, trails, and an education center. Eastern Screech and Great Horned Owls occur on the property throughout the year whereas Northern Saw-whet Owls are reported from late November through April.

Access: From Newtown Square drive west on State Route 3 for several miles (kilometers) to the junction with State Route 352. Turn south onto State Route 352 and continue a limited distance to Forge Road on the left. Turn left (east) onto Forge Road and continue to Painter Road. Turn right (south) onto Painter Road and continue to the arboretum entrance on the left. Enter (between dawn and dusk), park in areas provided, and seek additional owl watching or listening information at the education center. Then explore the area on foot — or surrounding roads at night via automobile — to see or hear owls.

Tennessee

FALL CREEK FALLS STATE PARK
(near Pikeville)

Owls Present: Great Horned and Barred.

Description: A splendid 15,777-acre natural area with deep ravines, spectacular waterfalls, and running waterways.

Access: From Pikeville follow State Route 30 west for about 15 miles (24 kilometers) to the turn south onto another road and follow signs to the park. Explore the area on foot.

PICKETT STATE PARK AND FOREST
(near Jamestown)

Owls Present: Barred.

Description: A 11,742-acre area of deep forested ravines.

Access: From Jamestown follow U.S. Route 127 north for 2.0 miles (3.2 kilometers) to the junction with State Route 154. Turn east onto State Route 154 and continue 14 miles (22.4 kilometers) to the park entrance. Directional signs lead to the park headquarters where additional information can be secured.

RADNOR LAKE NATURAL AREA
(near Nashville)

Owls Present: Eastern Screech, Great Horned, and Barred.
Description: A 770-acre natural area in which old fields, wooded hills and ravines, and marshes are located back from Radnor Lake.
Access: From Nashville drive south on U.S. Route 31 (Franklin Pike) for about 4.5 miles (7.2 kilometers) from the city limit to Otter Creek Road. Turn right and follow Otter Creek Road for 1.5 miles (2.4 kilometers) to Radnor Lake. Explore the surrounding area on foot.

REELFOOT NATIONAL WILDLIFE REFUGE
(near Tiptonville)

Owls Present: Barred.
Description: A 9,586-acre refuge containing marshes, cypress forest, swamp forest, and wooded bluffs along with parts of Reelfoot Lake. Barred Owls can be heard at night and sometimes during the day.
Access: From Tiptonville drive east on State Route 22 for about 9.0 miles (14.4 kilometers) to Samburg where the refuge headquarters is located. Obtain additional details there about suitable owl watching/listening sites including the Grassy Island Unit which is a productive area for owl watchers.

Texas
AMARILLO AREA

Owls Present: Burrowing.
Description: Short-grass plain on which Burrowing Owls occur in prairie dog towns.
Access: From Amarillo, in the Texas Panhandle, follow for varying distances either Interstate 40 eastward or westward, U.S. Route 87 northward, or Interstate 27 southward, as well as various side roads leading from these major highways, looking for prairie dog towns on the plain and the Burrowing Owls that frequently are associated with them.

ANAHUAC NATIONAL WILDLIFE REFUGE
(near Winnie)

Owls Present: Short-eared.
Description: A 9,836-acre area of coastal marshes, sloughs, ponds, and wet prairie in which Short-eared Owls sometimes are seen in winter.
Access: From Interstate 10 near Winnie, drive south on State Route 124 to its junction with Route 1985. Turn right (west) onto Route 1985 and continue a few miles to a gravel road on the left and follow it into the refuge.

BENTSEN-RIO GRANDE VALLEY
STATE PARK (near Mission)

Owls Present: Eastern Screech, Ferruginous Pygmy, and Elf.
Description: A 587-acre park containing dense lowland forest, chaparral, and related Rio Grande vegetation. Eastern Screech Owls and Elf Owls, and more rarely Ferruginous Pygmy Owls, can be searched for at night with flashlights since the park is always open.
Access: In mission follow 10th Street to U.S. Business Route 83. There turn left onto Business Route 83 and continue to Park Road 43, turn left onto that road, and drive 5 miles (8 kilometers) to the park.

BIG BEND NATIONAL PARK
(reached from Marathon)

Owls Present: Flammulated.
Description: A huge 700,000-acre park with varied habitat. Flammulated Owls call at night in Boot Canyon.
Access: From Marathon travel south on U.S. Route 385 for 85 miles (136 kilometers) to the park headquarters. Inquire there for directions to Boot Canyon and seek other park travel regulations and suggestions.

BUFFALO LAKE NATIONAL WILDLIFE
REFUGE (near Umbarger)

Owls Present: Burrowing.
Description: A 7,677-acre refuge containing fields and Buffalo Lake. Burrowing Owls occur amid a large Black-tailed

Prairie Dog town on the refuge and are located with ease.
Access: From Umbarger, in northwestern Texas, drive south
on Route 168 and continue 1.5 miles (2.4 kilometers) to the
refuge entrance. Enter the refuge, look for prairie dog
colonies, and check them for owls.

EISENHOWER PARK (near Houston)

Owls Present: Barred.
Description: A small park, near Lake Houston, in whose
woodland Barred Owls can be heard and/or seen.
Access: From Houston drive east on Interstate 10 for about 14
miles (22.4 kilometers) to Sheldon Road. Turn left (north)
onto Sheldon Road and continue on it for about 7 miles (11.2
kilometers) to its deadend with Garrett Road. Turn left onto
Garrett Road and continue another 1.9 miles (3 kilometers) to
Aqueduct Road. Turn right onto Aqueduct Road and continue to Eisenhower Park beside Lake Houston. Enter the
park (camping is permitted) and listen or look for owls.

GUADALUPE MOUNTAINS NATIONAL PARK (near Pine Springs)

Owls Present: Flammulated, Great Horned, and Spotted.
Description: A 250-acre coniferous forest in a Bowl at the
summit of Pine Top Mountain where owls often are heard at
night.
Access: From Pine Springs, drive east on U.S. Routes 62/180
for about 1 mile (1.6 kilometers) to the park information
station where maps of the area and bird finding details can be
obtained. Then drive west of Pine Springs to the Pine Springs
Campground, park there, and hike up a steep trail for 3 miles
(4.8 kilometers) to the rim of the Bowl (elevation 8,000 feet).
From there walk some 250 feet lower into the Bowl to seek or
hear owls.

HOGAN PARK (near Garden City)

Owls Present: Burrowing.
Description: An outdoor education center where Burrowing
Owls are found in spring. Look for the birds on the ground, on
fence posts, or on utility poles.
Access: From the junction of Interstate 20 and State Route
349 near Midland, drive west on Interstate 20 for 10 miles (16

kilometers) to Exit 136. Exit there and continue north on Fairgrounds Road (unmarked as you enter it) for 4 miles (6.4 kilometers) to Wadley Road. Turn west (left) onto Wadley Road and continue about 0.5 mile (0.8 kilometer) to the park entrance on the right. Enter, go to the Outdoor Learning Center, then explore trails looking for owls.

MACKENZIE STATE PARK (in Lubbock)

Owls Present: Burrowing.
Description: A prairie dog town, surrounded by a concrete wall, in which Burrowing Owls live. The best viewing months for adults and newly fledged young are July and August, but owls also can be seen during other months.
Access: The park is located in Lubbock northeast of the intersection of Fourth Street and Avenue A.

MEMORIAL PARK (in Houston)

Owls Present: Barred.
Description: A large park with extensive pine-oak forests in which Barred Owls are resident.
Access: From downtown Houston drive west on Memorial Drive to the park on the western side of the city.

MIDLAND AREA

Owls Present: Burrowing.
Description: A prairie dog town beside a road from which observations of owls can be made as they stand on mounds or look out from burrows in the mounds.
Access: From the junction of Interstate 20 and State Route 349 near Midland, drive west on Interstate 20 for approximately 9.5 miles (15.2 kilometers) to Exit 126. Leave Interstate 20 there and follow FM 1788 south for 4.4 miles (7 kilometers) to the prairie dog colony along the east side of the road. Continue slightly farther, turn around at a suitable spot, and return to the prairie dog colony to look for owls.

MULESHOE NATIONAL WILDLIFE REFUGE (near Muleshoe)

Owls Present: Burrowing.
Description: A 5,809-acre refuge of short grass rangeland,

rocky outcroppings, and several lakes. Burrowing Owls live in the various prairie dog towns on the refuge. Best owl watching is enjoyed during spring and summer.

Access: From Muleshoe drive south on State Route 214 for several miles to the refuge signs. Ask at the headquarters for the location of the best Burrowing Owl sites.

RITA BLANCA NATIONAL GRASSLANDS (near Dalhart)

Owls Present: Burrowing.

Description: A 77,000-acre grassland area separated into 38 units. Burrowing Owls occur in prairie dog towns on some of the units.

Access: From Dalhart, in the northwestern corner of the Panhandle, drive north on U.S. Route 385 for some miles to the grassland and explore the area for prairie dog towns and owls. For more details write to Rita Blanca National Grasslands, P.O. Box 38, Texline, Texas 79087.

WHITE MEMORIAL PARK (near Anahuac)

Owls Present: Barred.

Description: A 73-acre wooded park in which Barred Owls can be heard. Owls also are seen occasionally in the area on fence posts beside roads just before dark.

Access: At the junction of Interstate 10 and State Route 61, near Anahuac, drive south on State Route 61 for a very short distance to the park entrance on the right. Explore the park for owls.

Utah

BEAR RIVER MIGRATORY BIRD REFUGE (near Brigham City)

Owls Present: Short-eared.

Description: A 64,895-acre refuge at the mouth of the Bear River. A road on the top of a dike allows bird watchers to drive across part of the wetland area. Short-eared Owls nest on the refuge.

Access: From Brigham City turn west onto Forest Street from Main Street and follow it for 15 miles (24 kilometers) to the refuge headquarters where maps, information, and the latest bird finding details are available. Before entering the refuge register at the headquarters.

CAPITOL REEF NATIONAL PARK
(near Caineville)

Owls Present: Spotted.
Description: Narrow desert canyons in the Grand Wash section of the park. From April to June Spotted Owls sometimes can be located by listening for them after dark at the mouths of small side canyons.
Access: From Caineville, drive west on State Route 24 to the park entrance, then enter and follow signs to the Grand Wash region of the park. Check also with park authorities for other favorable owl finding locations.

SNOW BASIN SKI AREA (near Ogden)

Owls Present: Northern Saw-whet.
Description: Open meadows before you arrive at the ski area, where Northern Saw-whet Owls sometimes can be heard from March through May.
Access: From Ogden drive east on State Route 39 for about 10 miles (16 kilometers) to a U. S. Forest Service sign directing traffic south to the Snow Basin Ski Area. The large meadow just before the first turn-off to the ski area is the most likely spot for owl finding, but other open meadows nearby also may produce birds.

Vermont
MOUNT TOM (near Woodstock)

Owls Present: Great Horned and Barred.
Description: A 1,300-foot-high mountain covered with deciduous forest.
Access: From the Woodstock Inn, in the town of Woodstock, cross the Ottauquechee River, and follow Mountain Avenue to Falkner and French Memorial Parks. From there follow a trail to the top of Mount Tom. Listen for owls or attempt to call them up in this area.

Virginia

GREAT DISMAL SWAMP NATIONAL WILDLIFE REFUGE (near Suffolk)

Owls Present: Barred.
Description: A splendid 49,097-acre wilderness abounding in wildlife.
Access: In Suffolk, secure permission to drive along Jericho Ditch Lane at the refuge headquarters (200 North Main Street), then drive east on Washington Street to White Marsh Road which should be followed south for 0.75 mile (1.2 kilometers). Pass under a power line, then turn east and continue into the swamp. Other points of entry also are available. Secure details at the refuge headquarters. Listen for Barred Owls in various parts of the swamp.

OBSERVATORY HILL (in Charlottesville)

Owls Present: Barred.
Description: A mature deciduous forest on a hill on which the University of Virginia's observatory is located.
Access: In Charlottesville, drive west on McCormick Road and follow its winding course up Observatory Hill. Various foot trails, leading into the surrounding forest, can be used to search for, or listen to, owls.

Washington

IONE AREA

Owls Present: Great Gray, Northern Hawk, Northern Pygmy, and Barred.
Description: Meadows, coniferous forests, aspen-cottonwood woodland, etc. The general area is noted as an exceptionally productive winter area for rarer owl species.
Access: From Ione drive north on State Route 31 toward Mataline Falls, watching for owls in habitat adjacent to the highway. It also is worthwhile to explore other secondary roads in the area for owls.

KAMIAK BUTTE STATE PARK (near Pullman)

Owls Present: Great Horned, and Northern Pygmy.

Description: A butte, rising above the surrounding country-side, with rich coniferous-deciduous forest habitat.
Access: From Pullman, drive north on State Route 27 for about 11.5 miles (18.4 kilometers), then follow directional signs to the park.

SEATTLE

Owls Present: Snowy.
Description: The campus of the University of Washington as well as other parts of the city can harbor Snowy Owls during some winters.
Access: Maps of Seattle's streets are best used to seek out the university campus or other likely spots where owls might occur.

SKAGIT WILDLIFE RECREATION AREA
(near Conway)

Owls Present: Snowy and Short-eared.
Description: A 12,164-acre river delta and bay estuary. Winter owl watching is recommended.
Access: From Interstate 5 at Conway leave the highway, drive through Conway, cross a bridge over the south fork of the Skagit River, and continue west for 1.2 miles (1.9 kilometers) on Fir Island Road to Mann Road. Turn left onto Mann Road and drive south for 0.7 mile (1.1 kilometers) to the headquarters, then to nearby parking lots. Park and explore surrounding areas for owls.

SUN LAKES STATE PARK (near Coulee City)

Owls Present: Great Horned.
Description: High basaltic cliffs on the sides of the Lower Grand Coulee on which Great Horned Owls nest.
Access: From Coulee City, drive west on U.S. Route 2 for 2 miles (3.2 kilometers) to the junction with State Route 17, then turn south onto State Route 17 and continue for 4 miles (6.4 kilometers) to the park. Check cliffs near and within the park for owls.

Wisconsin
GRANT PARK (in Milwaukee)

Owls Present: Eastern Screech, Great Horned, and Long-eared.

Description: A large park with stands of spruce and pines in which owls roost. Clusters of spruce at the southern end of the park sometimes are particularly productive for owls.

Access: From downtown Milwaukee drive south on State Route 32 until it turns west, then continue south then east on South Lake Street to the park entrance. Explore much of the likely owl habitat in this large park on foot, taking care not to flush birds from roost trees.

HARRINGTON BEACH STATE PARK
(near Port Washington)

Owls Present: Short-eared.

Description: A natural area along the Lake Michigan shoreline in which owls stop during autumn and winter. The open area near the park entrance is the most likely spot to see the birds.

Access: From Port Washington drive north on U.S. Route 141 for 5.5 miles (8.8 kilometers) to the village of Lake Church. There turn east onto County Route D and continue to the parking area in the park.

MAZOMANIE BOTTOMS (near Mazomanie)

Owls Present: Great Horned and Barred.

Description: A public hunting area which is beside the Wisconsin River. Listen for owls which are resident in the area.

Access: From Mazomanie, in northwestern Dane County, drive north on County Route Y for about 4 miles (6.4 kilometers) to the point where the road makes a slight bend to the right. There turn left onto an unpaved road and continue to the next available left turn. Turn left there and continue to the end of the road. Park in a suitable spot, and walk along the trail at the chained gate. Barred Owls tend to occur in the trees along the trail; Great Horned Owls also occur in the area.

SUPERIOR AREA

Owls Present: Snowy.
Description: Open farmland along U.S. Route 2 between Superior and Brule. Snowy Owls sometimes appear in these fields during winter.
Access: From Superior drive along U.S. Route 2 en route to Brule, checking open fields along the way for owls.

WOODLAND DUNES NATURE CENTER
(near Manitowoc)

Owls Present: Short-eared and Northern Saw-whet.
Description: A wooded dune system along the Lake Michigan shoreline in which Northern Saw-whet Owls occur in autumn and Short-eared Owls occur during winter.
Access: In Manitowoc drive north on State Route 42 (Memorial Drive) to Woodland Drive. Turn left onto Woodland Drive and continue about 1.0 mile (1.6 kilometers) to Goodwin Drive. Trun right onto Goodwin Drive and continue to the nature center headquarters and trail entrance. Ask at the center for additional owl watching details, and the current status of owls in the area.

Canada

British Columbia
SEA ISLAND (near Vancouver)

Owls Present: Common Barn, Great Horned, Long-eared, and Short-eared; Snowy (in winter); Northern Saw-whet (occasionally).
Description: Sea Island is the site of the Vancouver International Airport and nearby sewage plant. Owls and other raptors hunt over exposed areas between the airport and the sewage plant.
Access: From Vancouver follow Route 993 to the airport road exit, then continue to the airport. Explore back roads on that part of Sea Island opposite the airport (the Iona Island area).

Manitoba

AGASSIZ PROVINCIAL FOREST AREA
(east of Winnipeg)

Owls Present: Northern Hawk and Great Gray.
Description: Roads bordered with boreal forest in and near Agassiz Provincial Forest. From mid-November to mid-April, Northern Hawk Owls and Great Gray Owls sometimes occur along these roads, perched on trees, poles, or other elevated objects.
Access: From Winnipeg drive east on Route 15 for about 25 miles (40 kilometers) to the Agassiz Provincial Forest. Then drive along roads in and near the forest, including Routes 11, 15, 44, 211, 214, and 307. Look for owls perched near the roads.

BELAIR PROVINCIAL FOREST AREA
(northeast of Winnipeg)

Owls Present: Northern Hawk and Great Gray.
Description: Roads bordered with boreal forest in the vicinity of Belair Provincial Forest. From mid-November to mid-April, Northern Hawk Owls and Great Gray Owls sometimes can be found along roads, perched on trees, poles, or other elevated objects.
Access: From Winnipeg drive northeast on Route 59 to its junction with Route 11 near Belair. Turn east onto Route 11 and follow it south to Lac du Bonnet. Alternatively, follow Route 304 north or south at its junction with Route 11. Look for owls along each of these roads.

CHURCHILL AREA (along Hudson Bay)

Owls Present: Snowy and Short-eared.
Description: Tundra surrounding the town of Churchill. Snowy Owls are common on the tundra during mid-April and May, whereas Short-eared Owls occur in wetland areas from mid-April to mid-October.
Access: Via railroad from Winnipeg or The Pas to Churchill, or via commercial airplane from Winnipeg or Thompson to Churchill. From Churchill to surrounding wildlife areas via foot, automobile, or taxi.

SANDILANDS PROVINCIAL FOREST AREA
(southeast of Winnipeg)

Owls Present: Northern Hawk and Great Gray.

Description: Roads bordered with boreal forest in the vicinity of Sandilands Provincial Forest. From mid-November to mid-April, Northern Hawk Owls and Great Gray Owls sometimes occur along roads, perched on trees, poles, or other elevated objects.

Access: From Winnipeg drive southeast on Route 1 to the junction with Route 308. Alternatively, from Sprague (near the Minnesota border) drive northwest on Route 12, or northeast on Route 308. Also explore Routes 203, 210, and 404 leading off Route 12 northwest of Sprague. Owls may be present along the sides of any of these roads.

WINNIPEG AREA

Owls Present: Snowy and Short-eared.

Description: From mid-October through April, Snowy Owls can occur perched on utility poles, fence posts, buildings, trees, and towers in open wind-swept fields southwest of Winnipeg. During summer and autumn, Short-eared Owls occur in wet meadow habitats southwest of Winnipeg.

Access: To find Snowy Owls, drive west or south of Winnipeg on Route 1, 2, or 3 as far as Route 34 (a north-south road) and various other north-south roads southwest of Winnipeg. Search likely habitats for owls. If seeking Short-eared Owls, search wet meadows just west and southwest of Winnipeg along Routes 247, 334, 412, and 424.

Newfoundland
LONG POINT AREA

Owls Present: Short-eared and Boreal.

Description: A 10.6-mile (17 kilometer)-long peninsula, known also as the Port-Au-Port Peninsula, along the southwestern side of Newfoundland, that funnels autumn migrants along its narrow width to the end at the Long Point Area. Short-eared Owls and Boreal Owls sometimes are seen in August and September along the side of the road.

Access: From Stephenville Crossing, follow local routes for about 10.6 miles (17 kilometers) to the Long Point Area and the peninsula tip. Additional directions and road information can be obtained in Stephenville Crossing or Stephenville.

NOTRE DAME BAY AREA

Owls Present: Snowy and Boreal.
Description: Bay coastlines, often isolated and remote, where Snowy Owls are found regularly during winter. Occasionally Boreal Owls also are reported during winter.
Access: This large bay, on Newfoundland's northeastern side, is serviced by Canada Route 1 and various feeder roads leading to small coastal villages along the bay. Any of the roads shown on road maps, leading to the bay shoreline, should be checked for owls.

Nova Scotia

SEAL ISLAND
(along the Yarmouth County Shore)

Owls Present: Short-eared.
Description: An island located off the southwestern end of Nova Scotia. Short-eared Owls are frequently seen during October.
Access: Seal Island is reached from various communities along the Yarmouth County shore of Nova Scotia. Further details are not available, but the island apparently is not difficult to reach.

Ontario

AMHERST ISLAND (near Kingston)

Owls Present: Common Barn, Eastern Screech, Great Horned, Snowy, Northern Hawk, Great Gray, Long-eared, Short-eared, Boreal, and Northern Saw-whet.
Description: An island on which large numbers of owls of many species winter during those winters when rodent populations are high. Under such conditions owl watching is exceptionally productive.
Access: From Watertown, New York, drive west on State Route 12E to the St. Lawrence River at Cape Vincent, New York. Cross the river there by ferry to Kingston, Ontario.

Then drive west on Route 33 to the ferry landing for Amherst Island.

GRAY DOE TRAIL HAWTHORN FIELD
(near Hamilton)

Owls Present: Eastern Screech, Great Horned, Long-eared, Boreal, and Northern Saw-whet.
Description: Small to medium White Pine trees that ring the southern end of an overgrown hawthorn field not far from forested valleys. Best owl watching (for Long-eared and Northern Saw-whet Owls) is from mid-October to early April with better than a 50 percent chance of finding Northern Saw-whet Owls.
Access: From the intersection of Plains Road West and Old Guelph Road in West Burlington, follow Old Guelph Road to a circular parking area adjacent to the arboretum and nature center operated by the Royal Botanical Gardens. Park there, then walk northwest across a large lawn to a trail that parallels railroad tracks for a short distance. Then continue on the trail across a smaller manicured area before entering the overgrown hawthorn field with pines along the southern edge in which owls are sometimes found. The walk along the trail is about 1 mile (1.6 kilometers) in length.

POINT PELEE NATIONAL PARK
(near Leamington)

Owls Present: Long-eared and Northern Saw-whet.
Description: An area of tangled bushes, red cedars, and hackberry woodland at the tip of the park adjacent to Lake Erie where owls sometimes roost. Best owl watching is from mid-October to early December.
Access: From Leamington drive south for about 6 miles (9.6 kilometers) into the park. Then continue south to the tip of the park where owls (especially Northern Saw-whet Owls) sometimes can be discovered roosting.

SULPHUR SPRINGS ROAD (near Ancaster)

Owls Present: Eastern Screech, Great Horned, and Long-eared (rarely).
Description: A road passing along an area of old fields and

hedgerows, and extending through mature mixed forest into the Dundas Valley to Sulphur Springs itself.

Access: From the fire hall and police station on the main road in Ancaster (just southwest of Hamilton) follow Church Street west for about 0.5 mile (0.8 kilometer) to Mineral Springs Road on the left. Begin there to listen for owls. Then continue along Mineral Springs Road and stop every 0.5 mile (0.8 kilometer) to listen for owls until you arrive at a "T" intersection. Turn right onto Sulphur Springs Road and drive about 0.25 mile (0.4 kilometer) to a lane on the right. Park at a suitable spot (a parking area is in a valley beyond the lane) and walk along the lane to the beginning of private property at the end. Alternatively, walk along a trail to the right of, and just north of, the parking area where the trail parallels a stream. Listen for owls at both sites.

UPPER MIDDLE ROAD OWL WOODS
(near Oakville)

Owls Present: Eastern Screech, Great Horned, Long-eared, Barred, and Northern Saw-whet.

Description: An area of fields and forest in which owls roost in white pines or in a red pine plantation. Best owl watching is done from mid-October to early April.

Access: From the Queen Elizabeth Highway between Hamilton and Toronto, drive north on Bronte Road North for about 1 mile (1.6 kilometers) to Upper Middle Road. Turn right, and immediately park near a dip in the road in a tiny valley. Then walk along the right (top) bank for about 0.25 mile (0.4 kilometer) to a pine plantation just above the valley or the White Pines in the valley below the plantation.

Quebec

CÔTE STE. CATHERINE SANCTUARY
(near Montreal)

Owls Present: Eastern Screech, Great Horned, Snowy, Long-eared, and Northern Saw-whet.

Description: The shoreline of the St. Lawrence River and Seaway in winter, or woodland in the park. Winter is best for finding Snowy Owls, autumn through spring for finding other woodland species.

Access: From the southern section of Montreal drive south across the Pont Champlain (toll bridge) then continue west on Quebec Route 132 to the third Brossard exit. There turn onto Marie Victorin Blvd. and continue several miles (kilometers) to signs for Côte Ste. Catherine Park. Follow the signs, cross the lift bridge over the St. Lawrence Seaway, then park in suitable spots and scan both sides of the river for Snowy Owls during winter. Eastern Screech, Great Horned, Long-eared, and Northern Saw-whet Owls also occur in woodland to the west but snowshoes or skies are needed to check this area in winter and rubber boots in spring and autumn.

ILE PERROT (near Montreal)

Owls Present: Eastern Screech, Great Horned, Snowy, Barred, Long-eared, Short-eared, Boreal, and Northern Saw-whet plus Northern Hawk Owl and Great Gray Owl during incursions.

Description: An island with hemlock and spruce woodlots, open fields, and roads. Great Horned, Barred, and Long-eared Owls occur regularly in hemlock and spruce woodland, Short-eared Owls hunt over fields in late winter and spring (especially along Don Quichotte Road), Snowy Owls occur on the island during winter when voles are abundant, and Boreal and Northern Saw-whet Owls may also occur during winter.

Access: From the western end of Montreal Island drive west on Route 20 to Ile Perrot and continue to the second traffic light. Turn onto Don Quichotte Road and follow it for several miles (kilometers) checking open fields along the way for Snowy or Short-eared Owls.

MONTREAL TO QUEBEC CITY AREA

Owls Present: Snowy.

Description: Fields along both sides of Route 20 during winter.

Access: From Montreal drive toward Quebec City on Route 20 remaining alert and looking for Snowy Owls near the highway.

MOUNT BRUNO (near Montreal)

Owls Present: Eastern Screech, Great Horned, Barred, Long-eared, Short-eared, Boreal, and Northern Saw-whet.
Description: A park in which Eastern Screech Owls occur in woodland near houses, Great Horned and Barred Owls can be heard in late winter and spring near a lake, Boreal (seen rarely) and Northern Saw-whet Owls use pine-cedar-hemlocks, and Long-eared and Short-eared Owls frequently roost in pines on a golf course in winter.
Access: From Montreal drive toward Quebec City on Route 20. At the junction of Routes 20 and 30 turn west onto Route 30 and continue to signs directing you to Parc Mont St. Bruno. Continue to the park. Explore various trails within the park checking appropriate habitat for various owl species.

MOUNT ROYAL (in Montreal)

Owls Present: Eastern Screech, Great Horned, Barred, Long-eared, Boreal, and Northern Saw-whet.
Description: A park within the city of Montreal. Eastern Screech Owls live in holes in trees, Great Horned and Barred Owls roost in taller evergreens during winter, Long-eared Owls sometimes appear in spring and autumn, and Northern Saw-whet and rarely Boreal Owls roost in cedars and spruce trees. September to November and March and April are the best months to check Mount Royal or the nearby Mount Royal Cemetery for owls.
Access: In Montreal, at the junction of CoDte des Neiges Road and Camillien Houde turn onto Camillien Houde, park in the second parking lot, then walk into the park or cemetery across the road from the park to search for owls.

NUN'S ISLAND (ILE DES SOEURS) AT MONTREAL

Owls Present: Eastern Screech, Great Horned, Snowy, Barred, Long-eared, Short-eared, Boreal, and Northern Saw-whet.
Description: An island, just south of Montreal, in the St. Lawrence River containing exposed shoreline, woodland, and open areas. November to March provides the best owl finding opportunities. Look for Eastern Screech, Great

Horned, Barred, and Long-eared Owls in woodland, Northern Saw-whet and rarely Boreal Owls in vines, Short-eared Owls in open areas on the western part of the island, and Snowy Owls along the island's shoreline.

Access: From Montreal drive south on Route 20 toward the Pont Champlain (toll bridge), but take the Nun's Island (Ile des Soeurs) exit just before reaching the bridge toll booths. Then drive to the end of Ile des Soeurs Blvd. and park. Explore the island on foot searching likely habitats for owls.

PHILIPSBURG SANCTUARY (near Philipsburg)

Owls Present: Great Horned and Barred.

Description: A bird sanctuary, through which trails extend, in which owls can be heard calling in late winter and early spring.

Access: From Philipsburg, near the Vermont border, drive south on Route 133 for about 0.5 mile (0.8 kilometer) and park at or near the Gaic Blue Motel. Then explore the sanctuary trails listening for owls.

VAUDREUIL-HUDSON-RIGAUD AREA

Owls Present: Snowy and Short-eared.

Description: Fence posts, utility poles, and isolated trees along or in open fields and farmland. Snowy Owls sometimes perch on such objects after arriving in the area between late November and April, and Short-eared Owls frequently can be found in the same areas.

Access: From Montreal drive west on Route 40 and continue on that route into the Vaudreuil-Hudson-Rigaud area. Once outside of Montreal, begin looking for owls as soon as open fields are encountered. Upon reaching the Vaudreuil area, explore local farm roads in the countryside including roads leading off Routes 201 and 340. A few owls usually are present in this section of Quebec each winter.

APPENDIX 1
ACCIDENTAL
NORTH AMERICAN
OWL SIGHTINGS

In addition to the owl species described earlier in this guide, the following species occurred accidentally in North America.

ORIENTAL SCOPS OWL *Otus sunia*

There are two records from the Aleutian Islands, Alaska.

MOTTLED OWL   *Ciccaba virgata*

There is one road-killed specimen from southern Texas along the Rio Grande.

APPENDIX 2
OWL
CONSERVATION
ORGANIZATIONS

In addition to the well-known national conservation organizations in Canada and the United States, all of which support the protection and conservation of owls and other birds of prey, the following organizations are especially concerned with owl and other raptor conservation. The list presented here is based, in part, upon information provided by the Raptor Information Center, The Raptor Research Foundation, Inc., and the Wildlife Information Center, Inc.

Alaska Raptor Rehabilitation Center
P.O. Box 2984
Sitka, AK 99835

Bird Rescue
200 East 11th Street
Weslaco, TX 78596

Carolina Raptor Center, Inc.
P.O. Box 16443
Charlotte, NC 28297-6443

Catskill Raptor Foundation
P.O. Box 633
Roscoe, NY 12776

Center for Birds of Prey
Florida Audubon Society
1101 Audubon Way
Maitland, FL 32751

Chattanooga Nature Center
Route 4, Garden Road
Chattanooga, TN 37409

Driftwood Research and Breeding Center for Owls
Site 57, Comp. 18
R.R. 2
Smithers, BC V0J 1N0, Canada

Five Mile Creek Raptor Center
P.O. Box 99098
Stockton, CA 95209-0098

George Miksch Sutton Avian Research Center, Inc.
P.O. Box 2007
Bartlesville, OK 74005-2007

Grounded Eagle Foundation, Inc.
H.C.R. 31, Box 900
Condon, MT 59826

Hawk Mountain Sanctuary Association
Route 2
Kempton, PA 19529

Liberty Wildlife Rehabilitation Foundation
11825 North 70th Street
Scottsdale, AZ 85254

Macdonald Raptor Research Centre of McGill University
21111 Lakeshore Road
Ste. Anne de Bellevue, PQ H9X 1C0, Canada

The Mews (Raptor Rehabilitation Center)
Cox Road
Portland, CT 06480

Midwest Raptor Rehabilitation Society, Inc.
P.O. Box 1812
Sioux City, IA 51102-1812

New Jersey Raptor Association
R.D. Box 440 J
Branchville, NJ 07826

Ohio State University Raptor Rehabilitation Program
Department of Veterinary Clinical Sciences
1935 Coffey Road
Columbus, OH 43210

Owl Rehabilitation Research Foundation
R. R. 1
Vineland Station, ON L0R 2E0, Canada

Prairie Raptor Project
Smoky Hills Audubon Society
R.R. 1
Tescott, KS 67484

Raptor Center
University of Minnesota
1920 Fitch Avenue
St. Paul, MN 55108

Raptor Center of Pueblo
5200 W. 11th Street
Pueblo, CO 81003

Raptor Education Foundation
925 East 17th Avenue, Suite 300
Denver, CO 80218

Raptor Information Center
National Wildlife Federation
1412 16th St., N. W.
Washington, DC 20036-2266

Raptor Rehabilitation Program
Colorado State University
Veterinary Teaching Hospital
Fort Collins, CO 80523

Raptor Research Foundation, Inc.
York College of Pennsylvania
Department of Biology
York, PA 17403-3426

Raptor Trust
1390 White Bridge Road
Millington, NJ 07946

Santa Cruz Predatory Bird Research Group
231 Clark Kerr Hall
University of California
Santa Cruz, CA 95064

Tyson Research Center
P.O. Box 193
Eureka, MO 63025

West Virginia Raptor Rehabilitation Center
P.O. Box 333
Morgantown, WV 26507

Wild Bird Rehabilitation Center
Audubon Park Zoo
P.O. Box 4327
New Orleans, LA 70178

Wildlife Information Center, Inc.
629 Green Street
Allentown, PA 18102

Wildlife Rescue, Inc.
4000 Middlefield Road
Palo Alto, CA 94303

Willowbrook Wildlife Haven
P.O. Box 2339
Glen Ellyn, IL 60138

APPENDIX 3
OWL PELLET
DATA FORM

Owl species: *Date:*

Roost location:

Pellet collector:

Pellet analysis by:

Pellet condition: Whole (   ) Partly broken (   ) Broken (   )

Pellet number	Pellet size (mm) Length/Width	Pellet weight (g.)	No. Prey Species in Pellet	Prey Species Identified in Pellet

SUGGESTED READING

The literature on owls is large and widespread. It is summarized well in a *Working Bibliography of Owls of the World* by Clark, Smith, and Kelso. The books listed below provide excellent additional reading about these fascinating and ecologically important birds.

ANGELL, T. 1974. *Owls*. University of Washington Press, Seattle, Wash.

AUSTING, G. R., and J. B. HOLT, JR. 1966. *The World of the Great Horned Owl*. J. B. Lippincott Co., Philadelphia, Pa.

BENT, A. C. 1938. *Life Histories of North American Birds of Prey*. Part 2. Bulletin 170. U.S. National Museum, Washington, D.C. (Reprinted by Dover Publications, Inc., New York, N.Y.)

BUNN, D. S., A. B. WARBURTON, and R. D. S. WILSON. 1982. *The Barn Owl*. Buteo Books, Vermillion, S.D.

BURTON, J. A. (ED.). 1973. *Owls of the World: Their Evolution, Structure, and Ecology*. E. P. Dutton & Co., Inc., New York, N.Y.

CLARK, R. J., D. G. SMITH, and L. H. KELSO. 1978. *Working Bibliography of Owls of the World*. Scientific and Technical Series 1. National Wildlife Federation, Washington, D.C.

CRAIGHEAD, J. J., and F. C. CRAIGHEAD, JR. 1956. *Hawks, Owls and Wildlife*. Stackpole Co., Harrisburg, Pa. (Reprinted by Dover Publications, Inc., New York, N.Y.)

DE LA TORRE, JULIO. 1990. *Owls: Their Life and Behavior*. Crown Publishers, Inc., New York, N.Y.

ECKERT, A. W., and K. E. KARALUS. 1973. *The Owls of North America*. Doubleday & Co., Inc., Garden City, N.Y.

HEINTZELMAN, D. S. 1979. *Hawks and Owls of North America.* Universe Books, New York, N.Y.

JOHNSGARD, PAUL A. 1988. *North American Owls: Biology and Natural History.* Smithsonian Institution Press, Washington, D.C.

MCKEEVER, K. 1980. *Care and Rehabilitation of Injured Owls.* Second Edition. W. F. Rannie, Publisher, Beamsville, Ontario, Canada.

NERO, R. W. 1980. *The Great Gray Owl.* Smithsonian Institution Press, Washington, D.C.

SPARKS, J., and T. SOPER. 1989. *Owls: Their Natural and Unnatural History.* Revised Edition. Facts On File, New York, N.Y.

SPRUNT, A., JR. 1955. *North American Birds of Prey.* Harper & Brothers, New York, N.Y.

TOOPS, CONNIE. 1990. *The Enchanting Owl.* Voyageur Press, Stillwater, Minn.

TYLER, H. A., and D. PHILLIPS. 1978. *Owls by Day and Night.* Naturegraph Publishers, Inc., Happy Camp, Calif.

VAN CAMP, L. F. 1975. *The Screech Owl: Its Life History and Population Ecology in Northern Ohio.* North American Fauna No. 71. U.S. Fish and Wildlife Service, Washington, D.C.

WALKER, L. W. 1974. *The Book of Owls.* Alfred A. Knopf, Inc., New York, N.Y.

INDEX

Page numbers in boldface type refer to illustrations.

Accidental Owl Sightings, 181
Aegolius
    acadicus, 24–25
    funereus, 23–24
Agassiz Provincial Forest Area
    (Manitoba), 172
Aitkin Area (Minn.), 132
Alaska Raptor Rehabilitation Center, 182
Amarillo Area (Texas), 162
Amherst Island (Ontario), 174–175
Anahuac National Wildlife Refuge
    (Texas), 163
Argonia Area (Kansas), 125
Asio
    flammeus, 21–23
    otus, 20–21
Athene cunicularia, 16–17
Aullwood Audubon Center (Ohio),
    149–150
Avon Area (N.Y.), 142

Back Cove (Maine), 127
Barn Island Wildlife Management
    Area (Conn.), 114
Bear River Migratory Bird Refuge
    (Utah), 166–167
Beaver Creek State Wildlife Area
    (Ohio), 150
Belair Provincial Forest Area
    (Manitoba), 172
Belfield Area (N.D.), 149
Beltrami Island State Forest Area
    (Minn.), 132
Beltsville Lake Area (Pa.), 155
Bentsen-Rio Grande Valley State
    Park (Texas), 163
Bignal Peak (N.M.), 140

Big Bend National Park (Texas),
    163
Bills, 49
Binoculars, 35
Bird Rescue, 182
Bitter Lake National Wildlife Refuge
    (N.M.), 140–141
Blackbird Creek (Del.), 117
Black Bottom Road (Md.), 129
Blue Ridge Parkway (N.C.), 147–148
Braddock Bay State Park (N.Y.),
    142
Bubo virginianus, 9–11
Buffalo Area (Okla.), 153
Buffalo Lake National Wildlife
    Refuge (Texas), 163–164
Buffalo Waterfront (N.Y.), 142–143
Burke Lakefront Airport (Ohio),
    150
Busch Memorial Wildlife Area
    (Mo.), 135

California Nature Preserve (Ohio),
    150
Campbell Falls State Park (Conn.),
    114
Camp Horseshoe (Pa.), 156
Cannonsville Reservoir Area
    (N.Y.), 143
Cape May Point (N.J.), 139
Capitol Reef National Park (Utah),
    167
Carolina Raptor Center, Inc., 182
Carpenter Park (Ill.), 122
Catskill Raptor Foundation, 182
Cave Creek Canyon (Ariz.), 106
Center for Birds of Prey, 182
Chattanooga Nature Center, 183

Cherry Creek Canyon (N.M.), 141
Cherry Creek Reservoir State Recreation Area (Colo.), 112–113
Cheyenne Bottoms State Wildlife Management Area (Kan.), 126
Chicago Area (Ill.), 122
Churchill Area (Manitoba), 172
Ciccaba virgata, 181
Cincinnati Nature Center (Ohio), 150–151
Color, 49
Conservation, 51–54
Conservation Organizations, 182–185
Corkscrew Swamp Sanctuary (Fla.), 118
Côte Ste. Catherine Sanctuary (Quebec), 176–177
Coxsackie Area (N.Y.), 143
Crab Orchard National Wildlife Refuge (Ill.), 122
Crane Creek State Park (Ohio), 151
Credit Island Park (Iowa), 124
Creve Coeur Lake (Mo.), 135
Croom Wildlife Management Area (Fla.), 118

Devil's Hopyard State Park (Conn.), 114
Diurnal Owl Watching, 27–28
Driftwood Research and Breeding Center for Owls, 183
Duluth (Minn.), 132–133

Eagle Point Park (Iowa), 124
Eastern Neck National Wildlife Refuge (Md.), 129
Eisenhower Park (Texas), 164
Elk Lake (N.Y.), 144
Englewood Reserve (Ohio), 151
Escambia River Swamp (Fla.), 118
Everglades National Park (Fla.), 119

Fall Creek Falls State Park (Tenn.), 161
Feathers, 48
Five Mile Creek Raptor Center, 183
Flashlight, 36
Fletcher Neck Area (Maine), 127–128
Fogelsville Pond (Pa.), 156
Food Habits, 41–42
Forest Glen County Preserve (Ill.), 123
Forest Lawn Cemetery (N.Y.), 144

Fort Hill State Memorial (Ohio), 151
Fort Klamath Area (Ore.), 154
Fort Rock State Monument (Ore.), 154

Gage Area (N.M.), 141
George Miksch Sutton Avian Research Center, Inc., 183
Gilgo Beach (N.Y.), 144
Glacier National Park (Mont.), 138
Glaucidium
   brasilianum, 14–15
   gnoma, 13–14
Glenwood Area (N.M.), 141
Goddard College Hawk and Owl Clinic, 182
Gooseberry Neck (Mass.), 130
Grand Island (N.Y.), 144
Grant Park (Wisc.), 170
Gray Doe Trail Hawthorn Field (Ont.), 175
Great Dismal Swamp National Wildlife Refuge (Va.), 168
Great Swamp National Wildlife Refuge (N.J.), 139
Greenlawn Cemetery (Ohio), 152
Grounded Eagle Foundation, Inc., 183
Guadalupe Mountains National Park (Texas), 164
Guilford Sluice (Conn.), 115
Guymon Area (Okla.), 153

Hambden Orchard Wildlife Area (Ohio), 152
Hammonasset State Park (Conn.), 115
Harrington Beach State Park (Wisc.), 170
Harrison Experimental Forest (Miss.), 134–135
Hastings Area (Minn.), 133
Hawk Mountain Sanctuary Assn., 183
Hearing, 48
Heart Lake (N.Y.), 145
Highbanks Metropolitan Park (Ohio), 152
Hogan Park (Texas), 164–165
Housatonic River Road (Conn.), 115–116
Hualapai Mountain Park (Ariz.), 106
Hunt-Wesson Hawk and Owl Preserve (Calif.), 109–110

Identification Plates, 56-103
Ile Perrot (Quebec), 177
Indiana Dunes National Lakeshore Area (Ind.), 123
Invasions, 44-46
Ione Area (Wash.), 168

Jamaica Bay Wildlife Refuge (N.Y.), 145
Jaybuckle Spring (Okla.), 153-154
Jones Beach State Park (N.Y.), 145
Jonesboro (Ark.), 108

Kamiak Butte State Park (Wash.), 168-169
Killdeer Plains Wildlife Area (Ohio), 152
Kissimmee Prairie (Fla.), 119
Kleber Wildlife Area (Ken.), 126
Kline's Run Park (Pa.), 156-157

Lake Jacomo County Park (Mo.), 136
Lake Placid Area (Fla.), 119
Leaser Lake (Pa.), 157
Lemhi River Valley Area (Idaho), 121
Lewis State Park (Pa.), 157
Liberty Wildlife Rehabilitation Foundation, 183
Lincoln's New Salem State Park (Ill.), 123
Little Creek Wildlife Area (Del.), 117-118
Long Point Area (Newfoundland), 173-174

Macdonald Raptor Research Centre of McGill University, 183
Mackenzie State Park (Texas), 165
Madera Canyon (Ariz.), 106-107
Mammal Identification Guides, 37
Mammoth Cave National Park (Ken.), 126
Manahawkin Fish and Wildlife Area (N.J.), 140
Martha's Vineyard (Mass.), 131
Mazomanie Bottoms (Wisc.), 170
Meadowlands Area (Minn.), 133
Medina to Steele Area (N.D.), 149
Memorial Park (Texas), 165
Mews, The (Raptor Rehabilitation Center), 183
Miami-Whitewater Forest County Park (Ohio), 153
Mianus River Park (Conn.), 116
Micrathene whitneyi, 15-16

Middle Creek Wildlife Management Area (Pa.), 157-158
Middle Patuxent Valley (Md.), 129-130
Midland Area (Texas), 165
Midwest Raptor Rehabilitation Society, Inc., 183
Migrations (Seasonal), 44
Mill Creek Park (Ohio), 153
Montauk Point Area (N.Y.), 146
Montreal-to-Quebec City Area (Quebec), 177
Mountain Lake Sanctuary (Fla.), 119
Mount Bruno (Quebec), 178
Mount Lemmon Area (Ariz.), 107
Mount Mitchell (N.C.), 149
Mount Pinos (Calif.), 110
Mount Royal (Quebec), 178
Mount Tom (Vermont), 167
Muleshoe National Wildlife Refuge (Texas), 165-166
Myakka River State Park (Fla.), 120

Nantucket (Mass.), 131
Nehantic State Forest (Conn.), 116
Nesting Owls, 33
Nest Structures, 51-54
New Bloomfield Area (Pa.), 158
New Jersey Raptor Association, 183
New Tripoli Area (Pa.), 158
Niagara Falls Airport (N.Y.), 146
Nockamixon State Park (Pa.), 158-159
Nocturnal Owl Watching, 28-32
North Platte Area (Neb.), 138
North Shore of Lake Superior (Minn.), 133-134
Notre Dame Bay Area (Newfoundland), 174
Noxubee National Wildlife Refuge (Miss.), 135
Nun's Island (Quebec), 178-179
Nyctea scandiaca, 11-12

Observatory Hill (Va.), 168
Ohio State University Raptor Rehabilitation Program, 183
Okefenokee Swamp (Ga.), 120-121
Orient Beach State Park (N.Y.), 146
Otus
  asio, 3-5
  flammeolus, 8-9

kennicottii, 5–6
sunia, 181
trichopsis, 7–8
Owl
  Barred, 18–19, **85**
  Boreal, 23–24, **99**
  Burrowing, 16–17, **81**
  Common Barn, 1–3, **57**
  Eastern Screech, 3–5, **59, 61, 63**
  Elf, 15–16, **79**
  Ferruginous Pygmy, 14–15, **79**
  Flammulated, 8–9, **67**
  Great Gray, 19–20, **45, 87, 89**
  Great Horned, 9–11, **69, 71**
  Long-eared, 20–21, **91, 93**
  Mottled, 181
  Northern Hawk, 12–13, **28, 75**
  Northern Pygmy, 13–14, **77**
  Northern Saw-whet, 24–25, **101, 103**
  Oriental Scops, 181
  Short-eared, 21–23, **29, 95, 97**
  Snowy, 11–12, **73**
  Spotted, 17–18, **83**
  Western Screech, 5–6, **65**
  Whiskered Screech, 7–8, **67**
Owl Pellet Data Form, 185
Owl Pellet Guide, 40
Owl Rehabilitation Research Foundation, 184

Peace Valley Park (Pa.), 159
Pearl River Wildlife Management Area (La.), 127
Pellet Bag, 37
Pellets, 39–41
Perch River Marsh (N.Y.), 147
Père Marquette State Park (Ill.), 123
Perkins Hill Road (Md.), 130
Philadelphia (Pa.), 159–160
Philipsburg Sanctuary (Quebec), 179
Phoenix Area (Ariz.), 107–108
Pickett State Park and Forest (Tenn.), 161
Pike National Forest (Colo.), 113
Pine Swamp Area (Pa.), 160
Pinnacle Mountain State Park (Ark.), 108–109
Pioneer Mothers Memorial Forest (Ind.), 124
Pioneers Park (Neb.), 138–139
Plum Island (Mass.), 131
Point Lobos Reserve State Park (Ca.), 111

Point Pelee National Park (Ont.), 175
Police Relations, 34
Popham Beach State Park (Maine), 128
Prairie Raptor Project, 184

Rachel Carson National Wildlife Refuge (Maine), 128
Radnor Lake Natural Area (Tenn.), 162
Raptor Center, 184
Raptor Center of Pueblo, 184
Raptor Education Foundation, 184
Raptor Information Center, 184
Raptor Rehabilitation Program, 184
Raptor Research Foundation, Inc., 184
Raptor Trust, 184
Reading Sign, 33–34
Red Lake Wildlife Management Area (Minn.), 134
Reed Memorial Wildlife Area (Mo.), 136
Reed Road Swamp (N.Y.), 147
Reedy Creek (Fla.), 120
Reelfoot National Wildlife Refuge (Tenn.), 162
Records, 36
Rita Blanca National Grasslands (Texas), 166
Rock Hill Area (Md.), 130
Rock Springs Park (Fla.), 120
Roosting Owls, 32–33
Roseau Area (Minn.), 134

Salton Sea National Wildlife Refuge (Ca.), 111
Sandilands Provincial Forest Area (Manitoba), 173
San Luis Valley (Colo.), 113
Santa Cruz Predatory Bird Research Group, 184
Santa Ynez Recreation Area (Calif.), 111
Sauvie Island Wildlife Management Area (Ore.), 154–155
Scarborough Marsh (Maine), 128
Schell-Osage Wildlife Management Area (Mo.), 136
Sea Island (B.C.), 171
Seal Island (Nova Scotia), 174
Seasonal Migrations, 44
Seattle (Wash.), 169
Shanks Wildlife Area (Mo.), 137

Sign, 33–34
Silhouettes, 30–31
Size, 49
Skagit Wildlife Recreation Area (Wash.), 169
Snake River Birds of Prey Natural Area (Idaho), 121–122
Snow Basin Ski Area (Utah), 167
South Beach State Park (Ore.), 155
Speotyto: see *Athene.*
Squaw Creek National Wildlife Refuge (Mo.), 137
St. Charles County Airport (Mo.), 137
Stewart Park (N.Y.), 147
Stone State Park (Iowa), 124–125
Strix
  nebulosa, 19–20
  occidentalis, 17–18
  varia, 18–19
Sulphur Springs Road (Ont.), 175–176
Sun Lakes State Park (Wash.), 169
Superior Area (Wisc.), 171
Surnia ulula, 12–13
Switzer Picnic Area (Ca.), 111–112
Synoptic Skull Collection, 38

Taberville Prairie (Mo.), 138
Talons, 49
Tape Recorder, 36
Telescope, 35
Tieg's Marsh (Iowa), 125
Tomales Bay State Park (Ca.), 112
Tyler Arboretum (Pa.), 161

Tyson Research Center, 184
Tyto alba, 1–3
Upper Middle Road Owl Woods (Ont.), 176

Vaca Key (Fla.), 120
Vaudreuil-Hudson-Rigaud Area (Quebec), 179
Village Creek State Park (Ark.), 109
Vision, 47–48

Waterford Beach (Conn.), 116
Weskeag Marsh (Maine), 128–129
West Virginia Raptor Rehabilitation Center, 185
Wetmore Area (Colo.), 113
Whitefish Point (Mich.), 131–132
White Memorial Foundation (Conn.), 117
White Memorial Park (Texas), 166
White River National Wildlife Refuge (Ark.), 109
Wild Bird Rehabilitation Center, 185
Wildlife Information Center, Inc., 185
Wildlife Rescue, Inc., 185
Willowbrook Wildlife Haven, 185
Winnipeg Area (Manitoba), 173
Woodland Dunes Nature Center (Wisc.), 171
Wright's Point (Ore.), 155

Yosemite National Park (Ca.), 112

A CATALOG OF SELECTED
DOVER BOOKS
IN ALL FIELDS OF INTEREST

A CATALOG OF SELECTED
DOVER BOOKS
IN ALL FIELDS OF INTEREST

DRAWINGS OF REMBRANDT, edited by Seymour Slive. Updated Lippmann, Hofstede de Groot edition, with definitive scholarly apparatus. All portraits, biblical sketches, landscapes, nudes. Oriental figures, classical studies, together with selection of work by followers. 550 illustrations. Total of 630pp. 9⅛ × 12¼.
21485-0, 21486-9 Pa., Two-vol. set $29.90

GHOST AND HORROR STORIES OF AMBROSE BIERCE, Ambrose Bierce. 24 tales vividly imagined, strangely prophetic, and decades ahead of their time in technical skill: "The Damned Thing," "An Inhabitant of Carcosa," "The Eyes of the Panther," "Moxon's Master," and 20 more. 199pp. 5⅜ × 8½. 20767-6 Pa. $4.95

ETHICAL WRITINGS OF MAIMONIDES, Maimonides. Most significant ethical works of great medieval sage, newly translated for utmost precision, readability. Laws Concerning Character Traits, Eight Chapters, more. 192pp. 5⅜ × 8½.
24522-5 Pa. $4.50

THE EXPLORATION OF THE COLORADO RIVER AND ITS CANYONS, J. W. Powell. Full text of Powell's 1,000-mile expedition down the fabled Colorado in 1869. Superb account of terrain, geology, vegetation, Indians, famine, mutiny, treacherous rapids, mighty canyons, during exploration of last unknown part of continental U.S. 400pp. 5⅜ × 8½. 20094-9 Pa. $7.95

HISTORY OF PHILOSOPHY, Julián Marías. Clearest one-volume history on the market. Every major philosopher and dozens of others, to Existentialism and later. 505pp. 5⅜ × 8½. 21739-6 Pa. $9.95

ALL ABOUT LIGHTNING, Martin A. Uman. Highly readable nontechnical survey of nature and causes of lightning, thunderstorms, ball lightning, St. Elmo's Fire, much more. Illustrated. 192pp. 5⅜ × 8½. 25237-X Pa. $5.95

SAILING ALONE AROUND THE WORLD, Captain Joshua Slocum. First man to sail around the world, alone, in small boat. One of great feats of seamanship told in delightful manner. 67 illustrations. 294pp. 5⅜ × 8½. 20326-3 Pa. $4.95

LETTERS AND NOTES ON THE MANNERS, CUSTOMS AND CONDITIONS OF THE NORTH AMERICAN INDIANS, George Catlin. Classic account of life among Plains Indians: ceremonies, hunt, warfare, etc. 312 plates. 572pp. of text. 6⅛ × 9¼. 22118-0, 22119-9, Pa., Two-vol. set $17.90

ALASKA: The Harriman Expedition, 1899, John Burroughs, John Muir, et al. Informative, engrossing accounts of two-month, 9,000-mile expedition. Native peoples, wildlife, forests, geography, salmon industry, glaciers, more. Profusely illustrated. 240 black-and-white line drawings. 124 black-and-white photographs. 3 maps. Index. 576pp. 5⅜ × 8½. 25109-8 Pa. $11.95

CATALOG OF DOVER BOOKS

THE BOOK OF BEASTS: Being a Translation from a Latin Bestiary of the Twelfth Century, T. H. White. Wonderful catalog of real and fanciful beasts: manticore, griffin, phoenix, amphivius, jaculus, many more. White's witty erudite commentary on scientific, historical aspects enhances fascinating glimpse of medieval mind. Illustrated. 296pp. 5⅜ × 8¼. (Available in U.S. only)   24609-4 Pa. $6.95

FRANK LLOYD WRIGHT: Architecture and Nature with 160 Illustrations, Donald Hoffmann. Profusely illustrated study of influence of nature—especially prairie—on Wright's designs for Fallingwater, Robie House, Guggenheim Museum, other masterpieces. 96pp. 9¼ × 10¾.   25098-9 Pa. $8.95

FRANK LLOYD WRIGHT'S FALLINGWATER, Donald Hoffmann. Wright's famous waterfall house: planning and construction of organic idea. History of site, owners, Wright's personal involvement. Photographs of various stages of building. Preface by Edgar Kaufmann, Jr. 100 illustrations. 112pp. 9¼ × 10.
23671-4 Pa. $8.95

YEARS WITH FRANK LLOYD WRIGHT: Apprentice to Genius, Edgar Tafel. Insightful memoir by a former apprentice presents a revealing portrait of Wright the man, the inspired teacher, the greatest American architect. 372 black-and-white illustrations. Preface. Index. vi + 228pp. 8¼ × 11.   24801-1 Pa. $10.95

THE STORY OF KING ARTHUR AND HIS KNIGHTS, Howard Pyle. Enchanting version of King Arthur fable has delighted generations with imaginative narratives of exciting adventures and unforgettable illustrations by the author. 41 illustrations. xviii + 313pp. 6⅛ × 9¼.   21445-1 Pa. $6.95

THE GODS OF THE EGYPTIANS, E. A. Wallis Budge. Thorough coverage of numerous gods of ancient Egypt by foremost Egyptologist. Information on evolution of cults, rites and gods; the cult of Osiris; the Book of the Dead and its rites; the sacred animals and birds; Heaven and Hell; and more. 956pp. 6⅛ × 9¼.
22055-9, 22056-7 Pa., Two-vol. set $21.90

A THEOLOGICO-POLITICAL TREATISE, Benedict Spinoza. Also contains unfinished *Political Treatise*. Great classic on religious liberty, theory of government on common consent. R. Elwes translation. Total of 421pp. 5⅜ × 8½.
20249-6 Pa. $7.95

INCIDENTS OF TRAVEL IN CENTRAL AMERICA, CHIAPAS, AND YUCATAN, John L. Stephens. Almost single-handed discovery of Maya culture; exploration of ruined cities, monuments, temples; customs of Indians. 115 drawings. 892pp. 5⅜ × 8½.   22404-X, 22405-8 Pa., Two-vol. set $17.90

LOS CAPRICHOS, Francisco Goya. 80 plates of wild, grotesque monsters and caricatures. Prado manuscript included. 183pp. 6⅜ × 9⅜.   22384-1 Pa. $5.95

AUTOBIOGRAPHY: The Story of My Experiments with Truth, Mohandas K. Gandhi. Not hagiography, but Gandhi in his own words. Boyhood, legal studies, purification, the growth of the Satyagraha (nonviolent protest) movement. Critical, inspiring work of the man who freed India. 480pp. 5⅜ × 8½. (Available in U.S. only)
24593-4 Pa. $6.95

ILLUSTRATED DICTIONARY OF HISTORIC ARCHITECTURE, edited by Cyril M. Harris. Extraordinary compendium of clear, concise definitions for over 5,000 important architectural terms complemented by over 2,000 line drawings. Covers full spectrum of architecture from ancient ruins to 20th-century Modernism. Preface. 592pp. 7½ × 9⅜. 24444-X Pa. $15.95

THE NIGHT BEFORE CHRISTMAS, Clement C. Moore. Full text, and woodcuts from original 1848 book. Also critical, historical material. 19 illustrations. 40pp. 4⅝ × 6. 22797-9 Pa. $2.50

THE LESSON OF JAPANESE ARCHITECTURE: 165 Photographs, Jiro Harada. Memorable gallery of 165 photographs taken in the 1930s of exquisite Japanese homes of the well-to-do and historic buildings. 13 line diagrams. 192pp. 8⅜ × 11¼. 24778-3 Pa. $10.95

THE AUTOBIOGRAPHY OF CHARLES DARWIN AND SELECTED LETTERS, edited by Francis Darwin. The fascinating life of eccentric genius composed of an intimate memoir by Darwin (intended for his children); commentary by his son, Francis; hundreds of fragments from notebooks, journals, papers; and letters to and from Lyell, Hooker, Huxley, Wallace and Henslow. xi + 365pp. 5⅜ × 8. 20479-0 Pa. $6.95

WONDERS OF THE SKY: Observing Rainbows, Comets, Eclipses, the Stars and Other Phenomena, Fred Schaaf. Charming, easy-to-read poetic guide to all manner of celestial events visible to the naked eye. Mock suns, glories, Belt of Venus, more. Illustrated. 299pp. 5¼ × 8¼. 24402-4 Pa. $8.95

BURNHAM'S CELESTIAL HANDBOOK, Robert Burnham, Jr. Thorough guide to the stars beyond our solar system. Exhaustive treatment. Alphabetical by constellation: Andromeda to Cetus in Vol. 1; Chamaeleon to Orion in Vol. 2; and Pavo to Vulpecula in Vol. 3. Hundreds of illustrations. Index in Vol. 3. 2,000pp. 6⅛ × 9¼. 23567-X, 23568-8, 23673-0 Pa., Three-vol. set $41.85

STAR NAMES: Their Lore and Meaning, Richard Hinckley Allen. Fascinating history of names various cultures have given to constellations and literary and folkloristic uses that have been made of stars. Indexes to subjects. Arabic and Greek names. Biblical references. Bibliography. 563pp. 5⅜ × 8½. 21079-0 Pa. $8.95

THIRTY YEARS THAT SHOOK PHYSICS: The Story of Quantum Theory, George Gamow. Lucid, accessible introduction to influential theory of energy and matter. Careful explanations of Dirac's anti-particles, Bohr's model of the atom, much more. 12 plates. Numerous drawings. 240pp. 5⅜ × 8½. 24895-X Pa. $6.95

CHINESE DOMESTIC FURNITURE IN PHOTOGRAPHS AND MEASURED DRAWINGS, Gustav Ecke. A rare volume, now affordably priced for antique collectors, furniture buffs and art historians. Detailed review of styles ranging from early Shang to late Ming. Unabridged republication. 161 black-and-white drawings, photos. Total of 224pp. 8⅜ × 11¼. (Available in U.S. only) 25171-3 Pa. $14.95

VINCENT VAN GOGH: A Biography, Julius Meier-Graefe. Dynamic, penetrating study of artist's life, relationship with brother, Theo, painting techniques, travels, more. Readable, engrossing. 160pp. 5⅜ × 8½. (Available in U.S. only) 25253-1 Pa. $4.95

HOW TO WRITE, Gertrude Stein. Gertrude Stein claimed anyone could understand her unconventional writing—here are clues to help. Fascinating improvisations, language experiments, explanations illuminate Stein's craft and the art of writing. Total of 414pp. 4⅝ × 6⅝.   23144-5 Pa. $6.95

ADVENTURES AT SEA IN THE GREAT AGE OF SAIL: Five Firsthand Narratives, edited by Elliot Snow. Rare true accounts of exploration, whaling, shipwreck, fierce natives, trade, shipboard life, more. 33 illustrations. Introduction. 353pp. 5⅜ × 8½.   25177-2 Pa. $9.95

THE HERBAL OR GENERAL HISTORY OF PLANTS, John Gerard. Classic descriptions of about 2,850 plants—with over 2,700 illustrations—includes Latin and English names, physical descriptions, varieties, time and place of growth, more. 2,706 illustrations. xlv + 1,678pp. 8½ × 12¼.   23147-X Cloth. $75.00

DOROTHY AND THE WIZARD IN OZ, L. Frank Baum. Dorothy and the Wizard visit the center of the Earth, where people are vegetables, glass houses grow and Oz characters reappear. Classic sequel to *Wizard of Oz*. 256pp. 5⅜ × 8.
24714-7 Pa. $5.95

SONGS OF EXPERIENCE: Facsimile Reproduction with 26 Plates in Full Color, William Blake. This facsimile of Blake's original "Illuminated Book" reproduces 26 full-color plates from a rare 1826 edition. Includes "The Tyger," "London," "Holy Thursday," and other immortal poems. 26 color plates. Printed text of poems. 48pp. 5¼ × 7.   24636-1 Pa. $3.95

SONGS OF INNOCENCE, William Blake. The first and most popular of Blake's famous "Illuminated Books," in a facsimile edition reproducing all 31 brightly colored plates. Additional printed text of each poem. 64pp. 5¼ × 7.
22764-2 Pa. $3.95

PRECIOUS STONES, Max Bauer. Classic, thorough study of diamonds, rubies, emeralds, garnets, etc.: physical character, occurrence, properties, use, similar topics. 20 plates, 8 in color. 94 figures. 659pp. 6⅛ × 9¼.
21910-0, 21911-9 Pa., Two-vol. set $15.90

ENCYCLOPEDIA OF VICTORIAN NEEDLEWORK, S. F. A. Caulfeild and Blanche Saward. Full, precise descriptions of stitches, techniques for dozens of needlecrafts—most exhaustive reference of its kind. Over 800 figures. Total of 679pp. 8⅛ × 11.   22800-2, 22801-0 Pa., Two-vol. set $23.90

THE MARVELOUS LAND OF OZ, L. Frank Baum. Second Oz book, the Scarecrow and Tin Woodman are back with hero named Tip, Oz magic. 136 illustrations. 287pp. 5⅜ × 8½.   20692-0 Pa. $5.95

WILD FOWL DECOYS, Joel Barber. Basic book on the subject, by foremost authority and collector. Reveals history of decoy making and rigging, place in American culture, different kinds of decoys, how to make them, and how to use them. 140 plates. 156pp. 7⅞ × 10¾.   20011-6 Pa. $8.95

HISTORY OF LACE, Mrs. Bury Palliser. Definitive, profusely illustrated chronicle of lace from earliest times to late 19th century. Laces of Italy, Greece, England, France, Belgium, etc. Landmark of needlework scholarship. 266 illustrations. 672pp. 6⅛ × 9¼.   24742-2 Pa. $16.95

ILLUSTRATED GUIDE TO SHAKER FURNITURE, Robert Meader. All furniture and appurtenances, with much on unknown local styles. 235 photos. 146pp. 9 × 12.   22819-3 Pa. $8.95

WHALE SHIPS AND WHALING: A Pictorial Survey, George Francis Dow. Over 200 vintage engravings, drawings, photographs of barks, brigs, cutters, other vessels. Also harpoons, lances, whaling guns, many other artifacts. Comprehensive text by foremost authority. 207 black-and-white illustrations. 288pp. 6 × 9.
24808-9 Pa. $9.95

THE BERTRAMS, Anthony Trollope. Powerful portrayal of blind self-will and thwarted ambition includes one of Trollope's most heartrending love stories. 497pp. 5⅜ × 8½.   25119-5 Pa. $9.95

ADVENTURES WITH A HAND LENS, Richard Headstrom. Clearly written guide to observing and studying flowers and grasses, fish scales, moth and insect wings, egg cases, buds, feathers, seeds, leaf scars, moss, molds, ferns, common crystals, etc.—all with an ordinary, inexpensive magnifying glass. 209 exact line drawings aid in your discoveries. 220pp. 5⅜ × 8½.   23330-8 Pa. $5.95

RODIN ON ART AND ARTISTS, Auguste Rodin. Great sculptor's candid, wide-ranging comments on meaning of art; great artists; relation of sculpture to poetry, painting, music; philosophy of life, more. 76 superb black-and-white illustrations of Rodin's sculpture, drawings and prints. 119pp. 8⅜ × 11¼.   24487-3 Pa. $7.95

FIFTY CLASSIC FRENCH FILMS, 1912–1982: A Pictorial Record, Anthony Slide. Memorable stills from Grand Illusion, Beauty and the Beast, Hiroshima, Mon Amour, many more. Credits, plot synopses, reviews, etc. 160pp. 8¼ × 11.
25256-6 Pa. $11.95

THE PRINCIPLES OF PSYCHOLOGY, William James. Famous long course complete, unabridged. Stream of thought, time perception, memory, experimental methods; great work decades ahead of its time. 94 figures. 1,391pp. 5⅜ × 8½.
20381-6, 20382-4 Pa., Two-vol. set $25.90

BODIES IN A BOOKSHOP, R. T. Campbell. Challenging mystery of blackmail and murder with ingenious plot and superbly drawn characters. In the best tradition of British suspense fiction. 192pp. 5⅜ × 8½.   24720-1 Pa. $4.95

CALLAS: Portrait of a Prima Donna, George Jellinek. Renowned commentator on the musical scene chronicles incredible career and life of the most controversial, fascinating, influential operatic personality of our time. 64 black-and-white photographs. 416pp. 5⅜ × 8¼.   25047-4 Pa. $8.95

GEOMETRY, RELATIVITY AND THE FOURTH DIMENSION, Rudolph Rucker. Exposition of fourth dimension, concepts of relativity as Flatland characters continue adventures. Popular, easily followed yet accurate, profound. 141 illustrations. 133pp. 5⅜ × 8½.   23400-2 Pa. $4.95

HOUSEHOLD STORIES BY THE BROTHERS GRIMM, with pictures by Walter Crane. 53 classic stories—Rumpelstiltskin, Rapunzel, Hansel and Gretel, the Fisherman and his Wife, Snow White, Tom Thumb, Sleeping Beauty, Cinderella, and so much more—lavishly illustrated with original 19th-century drawings. 114 illustrations. x + 269pp. 5⅜ × 8½.   21080-4 Pa. $4.95

SUNDIALS, Albert Waugh. Far and away the best, most thorough coverage of ideas, mathematics concerned, types, construction, adjusting anywhere. Over 100 illustrations. 230pp. 5⅜ × 8½. 22947-5 Pa. $5.95

PICTURE HISTORY OF THE NORMANDIE: With 190 Illustrations, Frank O. Braynard. Full story of legendary French ocean liner: Art Deco interiors, design innovations, furnishings, celebrities, maiden voyage, tragic fire, much more. Extensive text. 144pp. 8⅜ × 11¾. 25257-4 Pa. $10.95

THE FIRST AMERICAN COOKBOOK: A Facsimile of "American Cookery," 1796, Amelia Simmons. Facsimile of the first American-written cookbook published in the United States contains authentic recipes for colonial favorites—pumpkin pudding, winter squash pudding, spruce beer, Indian slapjacks, and more. Introductory Essay and Glossary of colonial cooking terms. 80pp. 5⅜ × 8½. 24710-4 Pa. $3.50

101 PUZZLES IN THOUGHT AND LOGIC, C. R. Wylie, Jr. Solve murders and robberies, find out which fishermen are liars, how a blind man could possibly identify a color—purely by your own reasoning! 107pp. 5⅜ × 8½. 20367-0 Pa. $2.95

ANCIENT EGYPTIAN MYTHS AND LEGENDS, Lewis Spence. Examines animism, totemism, fetishism, creation myths, deities, alchemy, art and magic, other topics. Over 50 illustrations. 432pp. 5⅜ × 8½. 26525-0 Pa. $8.95

ANTHROPOLOGY AND MODERN LIFE, Franz Boas. Great anthropologist's classic treatise on race and culture. Introduction by Ruth Bunzel. Only inexpensive paperback edition. 255pp. 5⅜ × 8½. 25245-0 Pa. $6.95

THE TALE OF PETER RABBIT, Beatrix Potter. The inimitable Peter's terrifying adventure in Mr. McGregor's garden, with all 27 wonderful, full-color Potter illustrations. 55pp. 4¼ × 5½. (Available in U.S. only) 22827-4 Pa. $1.75

THREE PROPHETIC SCIENCE FICTION NOVELS, H. G. Wells. *When the Sleeper Wakes, A Story of the Days to Come* and *The Time Machine* (full version). 335pp. 5⅜ × 8½. (Available in U.S. only) 20605-X Pa. $8.95

APICIUS COOKERY AND DINING IN IMPERIAL ROME, edited and translated by Joseph Dommers Vehling. Oldest known cookbook in existence offers readers a clear picture of what foods Romans ate, how they prepared them, etc. 49 illustrations. 301pp. 6⅛ × 9¼. 23563-7 Pa. $7.95

SHAKESPEARE LEXICON AND QUOTATION DICTIONARY, Alexander Schmidt. Full definitions, locations, shades of meaning of every word in plays and poems. More than 50,000 exact quotations. 1,485pp. 6½ × 9¼. 22726-X, 22727-8 Pa., Two-vol. set $31.90

THE WORLD'S GREAT SPEECHES, edited by Lewis Copeland and Lawrence W. Lamm. Vast collection of 278 speeches from Greeks to 1970. Powerful and effective models; unique look at history. 842pp. 5⅜ × 8½. 20468-5 Pa. $12.95

CATALOG OF DOVER BOOKS

THE BLUE FAIRY BOOK, Andrew Lang. The first, most famous collection, with many familiar tales: Little Red Riding Hood, Aladdin and the Wonderful Lamp, Puss in Boots, Sleeping Beauty, Hansel and Gretel, Rumpelstiltskin; 37 in all. 138 illustrations. 390pp. 5⅜ × 8½.   21437-0 Pa. $6.95

THE STORY OF THE CHAMPIONS OF THE ROUND TABLE, Howard Pyle. Sir Launcelot, Sir Tristram and Sir Percival in spirited adventures of love and triumph retold in Pyle's inimitable style. 50 drawings, 31 full-page. xviii + 329pp. 6½ × 9¼.   21883-X Pa. $7.95

THE MYTHS OF THE NORTH AMERICAN INDIANS, Lewis Spence. Myths and legends of the Algonquins, Iroquois, Pawnees and Sioux with comprehensive historical and ethnological commentary. 36 illustrations. 5⅜ × 8½.
25967-6 Pa. $8.95

GREAT DINOSAUR HUNTERS AND THEIR DISCOVERIES, Edwin H. Colbert. Fascinating, lavishly illustrated chronicle of dinosaur research, 1820s to 1960. Achievements of Cope, Marsh, Brown, Buckland, Mantell, Huxley, many others. 384pp. 5¼ × 8¼.   24701-5 Pa. $7.95

THE TASTEMAKERS, Russell Lynes. Informal, illustrated social history of American taste 1850s–1950s. First popularized categories Highbrow, Lowbrow, Middlebrow. 129 illustrations. New (1979) afterword. 384pp. 6 × 9.
23993-4 Pa. $8.95

DOUBLE CROSS PURPOSES, Ronald A. Knox. A treasure hunt in the Scottish Highlands, an old map, unidentified corpse, surprise discoveries keep reader guessing in this cleverly intricate tale of financial skullduggery. 2 black-and-white maps. 320pp. 5⅜ × 8½. (Available in U.S. only)   25032-6 Pa. $6.95

AUTHENTIC VICTORIAN DECORATION AND ORNAMENTATION IN FULL COLOR: 46 Plates from "Studies in Design," Christopher Dresser. Superb full-color lithographs reproduced from rare original portfolio of a major Victorian designer. 48pp. 9¼ × 12¼.   25083-0 Pa. $7.95

PRIMITIVE ART, Franz Boas. Remains the best text ever prepared on subject, thoroughly discussing Indian, African, Asian, Australian, and, especially, Northern American primitive art. Over 950 illustrations show ceramics, masks, totem poles, weapons, textiles, paintings, much more. 376pp. 5⅜ × 8. 20025-6 Pa. $7.95

SIDELIGHTS ON RELATIVITY, Albert Einstein. Unabridged republication of two lectures delivered by the great physicist in 1920–21. *Ether and Relativity* and *Geometry and Experience*. Elegant ideas in nonmathematical form, accessible to intelligent layman. vi + 56pp. 5⅜ × 8½.   24511-X Pa. $3.95

THE WIT AND HUMOR OF OSCAR WILDE, edited by Alvin Redman. More than 1,000 ripostes, paradoxes, wisecracks: Work is the curse of the drinking classes, I can resist everything except temptation, etc. 258pp. 5⅜ × 8½.   20602-5 Pa. $4.95

ADVENTURES WITH A MICROSCOPE, Richard Headstrom. 59 adventures with clothing fibers, protozoa, ferns and lichens, roots and leaves, much more. 142 illustrations. 232pp. 5⅜ × 8½.   23471-1 Pa. $3.95

PLANTS OF THE BIBLE, Harold N. Moldenke and Alma L. Moldenke. Standard reference to all 230 plants mentioned in Scriptures. Latin name, biblical reference, uses, modern identity, much more. Unsurpassed encyclopedic resource for scholars, botanists, nature lovers, students of Bible. Bibliography. Indexes. 123 black-and-white illustrations. 384pp. 6 × 9. 25069-5 Pa. $8.95

FAMOUS AMERICAN WOMEN: A Biographical Dictionary from Colonial Times to the Present, Robert McHenry, ed. From Pocahontas to Rosa Parks, 1,035 distinguished American women documented in separate biographical entries. Accurate, up-to-date data, numerous categories, spans 400 years. Indices. 493pp. 6½ × 9¼. 24523-3 Pa. $10.95

THE FABULOUS INTERIORS OF THE GREAT OCEAN LINERS IN HISTORIC PHOTOGRAPHS, William H. Miller, Jr. Some 200 superb photographs capture exquisite interiors of world's great "floating palaces"—1890s to 1980s: *Titanic, Ile de France, Queen Elizabeth, United States, Europa,* more. Approx. 200 black-and-white photographs. Captions. Text. Introduction. 160pp. 8⅞ × 11¾. 24756-2 Pa. $9.95

THE GREAT LUXURY LINERS, 1927-1954: A Photographic Record, William H. Miller, Jr. Nostalgic tribute to heyday of ocean liners. 186 photos of *Ile de France, Normandie, Leviathan, Queen Elizabeth, United States,* many others. Interior and exterior views. Introduction. Captions. 160pp. 9 × 12. 24056-8 Pa. $10.95

A NATURAL HISTORY OF THE DUCKS, John Charles Phillips. Great landmark of ornithology offers complete detailed coverage of nearly 200 species and subspecies of ducks: gadwall, sheldrake, merganser, pintail, many more. 74 full-color plates, 102 black-and-white. Bibliography. Total of 1,920pp. 8⅝ × 11¼. 25141-1, 25142-X Cloth., Two-vol. set $100.00

THE SEAWEED HANDBOOK: An Illustrated Guide to Seaweeds from North Carolina to Canada, Thomas F. Lee. Concise reference covers 78 species. Scientific and common names, habitat, distribution, more. Finding keys for easy identification. 224pp. 5⅜ × 8½. 25215-9 Pa. $6.95

THE TEN BOOKS OF ARCHITECTURE: The 1755 Leoni Edition, Leon Battista Alberti. Rare classic helped introduce the glories of ancient architecture to the Renaissance. 68 black-and-white plates. 336pp. 8⅜ × 11¼. 25239-6 Pa. $14.95

MISS MACKENZIE, Anthony Trollope. Minor masterpieces by Victorian master unmasks many truths about life in 19th-century England. First inexpensive edition in years. 392pp. 5⅜ × 8½. 25201-9 Pa. $8.95

THE RIME OF THE ANCIENT MARINER, Gustave Doré, Samuel Taylor Coleridge. Dramatic engravings considered by many to be his greatest work. The terrifying space of the open sea, the storms and whirlpools of an unknown ocean, the ice of Antarctica, more—all rendered in a powerful, chilling manner. Full text. 38 plates. 77pp. 9¼ × 12. 22305-1 Pa. $4.95

THE EXPEDITIONS OF ZEBULON MONTGOMERY PIKE, Zebulon Montgomery Pike. Fascinating firsthand accounts (1805-6) of exploration of Mississippi River, Indian wars, capture by Spanish dragoons, much more. 1,088pp. 5⅜ × 8½. 25254-X, 25255-8 Pa., Two-vol. set $25.90

CATALOG OF DOVER BOOKS

A CONCISE HISTORY OF PHOTOGRAPHY: Third Revised Edition, Helmut Gernsheim. Best one-volume history—camera obscura, photochemistry, daguerreotypes, evolution of cameras, film, more. Also artistic aspects—landscape, portraits, fine art, etc. 281 black-and-white photographs. 26 in color. 176pp. 8⅜ × 11¼.
25128-4 Pa. $14.95

THE DORÉ BIBLE ILLUSTRATIONS, Gustave Doré. 241 detailed plates from the Bible: the Creation scenes, Adam and Eve, Flood, Babylon, battle sequences, life of Jesus, etc. Each plate is accompanied by the verses from the King James version of the Bible. 241pp. 9 × 12. 23004-X Pa. $9.95

WANDERINGS IN WEST AFRICA, Richard F. Burton. Great Victorian scholar/adventurer's invaluable descriptions of African tribal rituals, fetishism, culture, art, much more. Fascinating 19th-century account. 624pp. 5⅜ × 8½. 26890-X Pa. $12.95

FLATLAND, E. A. Abbott. Intriguing and enormously popular science-fiction classic explores the complexities of trying to survive as a two-dimensional being in a three-dimensional world. Amusingly illustrated by the author. 16 illustrations. 103pp. 5⅜ × 8½. 20001-9 Pa. $2.50

THE HISTORY OF THE LEWIS AND CLARK EXPEDITION, Meriwether Lewis and William Clark, edited by Elliott Coues. Classic edition of Lewis and Clark's day-by-day journals that later became the basis for U.S. claims to Oregon and the West. Accurate and invaluable geographical, botanical, biological, meteorological and anthropological material. Total of 1,508pp. 5⅜ × 8½.
21268-8, 21269-6, 21270-X Pa., Three-vol. set $29.85

LANGUAGE, TRUTH AND LOGIC, Alfred J. Ayer. Famous, clear introduction to Vienna, Cambridge schools of Logical Positivism. Role of philosophy, elimination of metaphysics, nature of analysis, etc. 160pp. 5⅜ × 8½. (Available in U.S. and Canada only) 20010-8 Pa. $3.95

MATHEMATICS FOR THE NONMATHEMATICIAN, Morris Kline. Detailed, college-level treatment of mathematics in cultural and historical context, with numerous exercises. For liberal arts students. Preface. Recommended Reading Lists. Tables. Index. Numerous black-and-white figures. xvi + 641pp. 5⅜ × 8½.
24823-2 Pa. $11.95

HANDBOOK OF PICTORIAL SYMBOLS, Rudolph Modley. 3,250 signs and symbols, many systems in full; official or heavy commercial use. Arranged by subject. Most in Pictorial Archive series. 143pp. 8⅛ × 11. 23357-X Pa. $7.95

INCIDENTS OF TRAVEL IN YUCATAN, John L. Stephens. Classic (1843) exploration of jungles of Yucatan, looking for evidences of Maya civilization. Travel adventures, Mexican and Indian culture, etc. Total of 669pp. 5⅜ × 8½.
20926-1, 20927-X Pa., Two-vol. set $11.90

DEGAS: An Intimate Portrait, Ambroise Vollard. Charming, anecdotal memoir by famous art dealer of one of the greatest 19th-century French painters. 14 black-and-white illustrations. Introduction by Harold L. Van Doren. 96pp. 5⅜ × 8½.
25131-4 Pa. $4.95

PERSONAL NARRATIVE OF A PILGRIMAGE TO AL-MADINAH AND MECCAH, Richard F. Burton. Great travel classic by remarkably colorful personality. Burton, disguised as a Moroccan, visited sacred shrines of Islam, narrowly escaping death. 47 illustrations. 959pp. 5⅜ × 8½.
21217-3, 21218-1 Pa., Two-vol. set $19.90

PHRASE AND WORD ORIGINS, A. H. Holt. Entertaining, reliable, modern study of more than 1,200 colorful words, phrases, origins and histories. Much unexpected information. 254pp. 5⅜ × 8½.
20758-7 Pa. $5.95

THE RED THUMB MARK, R. Austin Freeman. In this first Dr. Thorndyke case, the great scientific detective draws fascinating conclusions from the nature of a single fingerprint. Exciting story, authentic science. 320pp. 5⅜ × 8½. (Available in U.S. only)
25210-8 Pa. $6.95

AN EGYPTIAN HIEROGLYPHIC DICTIONARY, E. A. Wallis Budge. Monumental work containing about 25,000 words or terms that occur in texts ranging from 3000 B.C. to 600 A.D. Each entry consists of a transliteration of the word, the word in hieroglyphs, and the meaning in English. 1,314pp. 6⅜ × 10.
23615-3, 23616-1 Pa., Two-vol. set $35.90

THE COMPLEAT STRATEGYST: Being a Primer on the Theory of Games of Strategy, J. D. Williams. Highly entertaining classic describes, with many illustrated examples, how to select best strategies in conflict situations. Prefaces. Appendices. xvi + 268pp. 5⅜ × 8½.
25101-2 Pa. $6.95

THE ROAD TO OZ, L. Frank Baum. Dorothy meets the Shaggy Man, little Button-Bright and the Rainbow's beautiful daughter in this delightful trip to the magical Land of Oz. 272pp. 5⅜ × 8.
25208-6 Pa. $5.95

POINT AND LINE TO PLANE, Wassily Kandinsky. Seminal exposition of role of point, line, other elements in nonobjective painting. Essential to understanding 20th-century art. 127 illustrations. 192pp. 6½ × 9¼.
23808-3 Pa. $5.95

LADY ANNA, Anthony Trollope. Moving chronicle of Countess Lovel's bitter struggle to win for herself and daughter Anna their rightful rank and fortune—perhaps at cost of sanity itself. 384pp. 5⅜ × 8½.
24669-8 Pa. $8.95

EGYPTIAN MAGIC, E. A. Wallis Budge. Sums up all that is known about magic in Ancient Egypt: the role of magic in controlling the gods, powerful amulets that warded off evil spirits, scarabs of immortality, use of wax images, formulas and spells, the secret name, much more. 253pp. 5⅜ × 8½.
22681-6 Pa. $4.50

THE DANCE OF SIVA, Ananda Coomaraswamy. Preeminent authority unfolds the vast metaphysic of India: the revelation of her art, conception of the universe, social organization, etc. 27 reproductions of art masterpieces. 192pp. 5⅜ × 8½.
24817-8 Pa. $6.95

CHRISTMAS CUSTOMS AND TRADITIONS, Clement A. Miles. Origin, evolution, significance of religious, secular practices. Caroling, gifts, yule logs, much more. Full, scholarly yet fascinating; non-sectarian. 400pp. 5⅜ × 8½.
23354-5 Pa. $6.95

THE HUMAN FIGURE IN MOTION, Eadweard Muybridge. More than 4,500 stopped-action photos, in action series, showing undraped men, women, children jumping, lying down, throwing, sitting, wrestling, carrying, etc. 390pp. 7⅞ × 10⅝.
20204-6 Cloth. $24.95

THE MAN WHO WAS THURSDAY, Gilbert Keith Chesterton. Witty, fast-paced novel about a club of anarchists in turn-of-the-century London. Brilliant social, religious, philosophical speculations. 128pp. 5⅜ × 8½.
25121-7 Pa. $3.95

A CÉZANNE SKETCHBOOK: Figures, Portraits, Landscapes and Still Lifes, Paul Cézanne. Great artist experiments with tonal effects, light, mass, other qualities in over 100 drawings. A revealing view of developing master painter, precursor of Cubism. 102 black-and-white illustrations. 144pp. 8¾ × 6⅝.
24790-2 Pa. $6.95

AN ENCYCLOPEDIA OF BATTLES: Accounts of Over 1,560 Battles from 1479 B.C. to the Present, David Eggenberger. Presents essential details of every major battle in recorded history, from the first battle of Megiddo in 1479 B.C. to Grenada in 1984. List of Battle Maps. New Appendix covering the years 1967–1984. Index. 99 illustrations. 544pp. 6½ × 9¼.
24913-1 Pa. $14.95

AN ETYMOLOGICAL DICTIONARY OF MODERN ENGLISH, Ernest Weekley. Richest, fullest work, by foremost British lexicographer. Detailed word histories. Inexhaustible. Total of 856pp. 6½ × 9¼.
21873-2, 21874-0 Pa., Two-vol. set $19.90

WEBSTER'S AMERICAN MILITARY BIOGRAPHIES, edited by Robert McHenry. Over 1,000 figures who shaped 3 centuries of American military history. Detailed biographies of Nathan Hale, Douglas MacArthur, Mary Hallaren, others. Chronologies of engagements, more. Introduction. Addenda. 1,033 entries in alphabetical order. xi + 548pp. 6½ × 9¼. (Available in U.S. only)
24758-9 Pa. $13.95

LIFE IN ANCIENT EGYPT, Adolf Erman. Detailed older account, with much not in more recent books: domestic life, religion, magic, medicine, commerce, and whatever else needed for complete picture. Many illustrations. 597pp. 5⅜ × 8½.
22632-8 Pa. $8.95

HISTORIC COSTUME IN PICTURES, Braun & Schneider. Over 1,450 costumed figures shown, covering a wide variety of peoples: kings, emperors, nobles, priests, servants, soldiers, scholars, townsfolk, peasants, merchants, courtiers, cavaliers, and more. 256pp. 8⅜ × 11¼.
23150-X Pa. $9.95

THE NOTEBOOKS OF LEONARDO DA VINCI, edited by J. P. Richter. Extracts from manuscripts reveal great genius; on painting, sculpture, anatomy, sciences, geography, etc. Both Italian and English. 186 ms. pages reproduced, plus 500 additional drawings, including studies for *Last Supper, Sforza* monument, etc. 860pp. 7⅞ × 10¾. (Available in U.S. only) 22572-0, 22573-9 Pa., Two-vol. set $31.90

THE ART NOUVEAU STYLE BOOK OF ALPHONSE MUCHA: All 72 Plates from "Documents Décoratifs" in Original Color, Alphonse Mucha. Rare copyright-free design portfolio by high priest of Art Nouveau. Jewelry, wallpaper, stained glass, furniture, figure studies, plant and animal motifs, etc. Only complete one-volume edition. 80pp. 9⅜ × 12¼. 24044-4 Pa. $10.95

ANIMALS: 1,419 Copyright-Free Illustrations of Mammals, Birds, Fish, Insects, Etc., edited by Jim Harter. Clear wood engravings present, in extremely lifelike poses, over 1,000 species of animals. One of the most extensive pictorial sourcebooks of its kind. Captions. Index. 284pp. 9 × 12. 23766-4 Pa. $10.95

OBELISTS FLY HIGH, C. Daly King. Masterpiece of American detective fiction, long out of print, involves murder on a 1935 transcontinental flight—"a very thrilling story"—NY Times. Unabridged and unaltered republication of the edition published by William Collins Sons & Co. Ltd., London, 1935. 288pp. 5⅜ × 8½. (Available in U.S. only) 25036-9 Pa. $5.95

VICTORIAN AND EDWARDIAN FASHION: A Photographic Survey, Alison Gernsheim. First fashion history completely illustrated by contemporary photographs. Full text plus 235 photos, 1840–1914, in which many celebrities appear. 240pp. 6½ × 9¼. 24205-6 Pa. $8.95

THE ART OF THE FRENCH ILLUSTRATED BOOK, 1700–1914, Gordon N. Ray. Over 630 superb book illustrations by Fragonard, Delacroix, Daumier, Doré, Grandville, Manet, Mucha, Steinlen, Toulouse-Lautrec and many others. Preface. Introduction. 633 halftones. Indices of artists, authors & titles, binders and provenances. Appendices. Bibliography. 608pp. 8⅜ × 11¼. 25086-5 Pa. $24.95

THE WONDERFUL WIZARD OF OZ, L. Frank Baum. Facsimile in full color of America's finest children's classic. 143 illustrations by W. W. Denslow. 267pp. 5⅜ × 8½. 20691-2 Pa. $7.95

FOLLOWING THE EQUATOR: A Journey Around the World, Mark Twain. Great writer's 1897 account of circumnavigating the globe by steamship. Ironic humor, keen observations, vivid and fascinating descriptions of exotic places. 197 illustrations. 720pp. 5⅜ × 8½. 26113-1 Pa. $15.95

THE FRIENDLY STARS, Martha Evans Martin & Donald Howard Menzel. Classic text marshalls the stars together in an engaging, nontechnical survey, presenting them as sources of beauty in night sky. 23 illustrations. Foreword. 2 star charts. Index. 147pp. 5⅜ × 8½. 21099-5 Pa. $3.95

FADS AND FALLACIES IN THE NAME OF SCIENCE, Martin Gardner. Fair, witty appraisal of cranks, quacks, and quackeries of science and pseudoscience: hollow earth, Velikovsky, orgone energy, Dianetics, flying saucers, Bridey Murphy, food and medical fads, etc. Revised, expanded In the Name of Science. "A very able and even-tempered presentation."—The New Yorker. 363pp. 5⅜ × 8. 20394-8 Pa. $6.95

ANCIENT EGYPT: Its Culture and History, J. E. Manchip White. From predynastics through Ptolemies: society, history, political structure, religion, daily life, literature, cultural heritage. 48 plates. 217pp. 5⅜ × 8½. 22548-8 Pa. $5.95

SIR HARRY HOTSPUR OF HUMBLETHWAITE, Anthony Trollope. Incisive, unconventional psychological study of a conflict between a wealthy baronet, his idealistic daughter, and their scapegrace cousin. The 1870 novel in its first inexpensive edition in years. 250pp. 5⅜ × 8½. 24953-0 Pa. $6.95

LASERS AND HOLOGRAPHY, Winston E. Kock. Sound introduction to burgeoning field, expanded (1981) for second edition. Wave patterns, coherence, lasers, diffraction, zone plates, properties of holograms, recent advances. 84 illustrations. 160pp. 5⅜ × 8¼. (Except in United Kingdom) 24041-X Pa. $3.95

INTRODUCTION TO ARTIFICIAL INTELLIGENCE: Second, Enlarged Edition, Philip C. Jackson, Jr. Comprehensive survey of artificial intelligence—the study of how machines (computers) can be made to act intelligently. Includes introductory and advanced material. Extensive notes updating the main text. 132 black-and-white illustrations. 512pp. 5⅜ × 8½. 24864-X Pa. $10.95

HISTORY OF INDIAN AND INDONESIAN ART, Ananda K. Coomaraswamy. Over 400 illustrations illuminate classic study of Indian art from earliest Harappa finds to early 20th century. Provides philosophical, religious and social insights. 304pp. 6⅜ × 9⅜. 25005-9 Pa. $11.95

THE GOLEM, Gustav Meyrink. Most famous supernatural novel in modern European literature, set in Ghetto of Old Prague around 1890. Compelling story of mystical experiences, strange transformations, profound terror. 13 black-and-white illustrations. 224pp. 5⅜ × 8½. (Available in U.S. only) 25025-3 Pa. $6.95

PICTORIAL ENCYCLOPEDIA OF HISTORIC ARCHITECTURAL PLANS, DETAILS AND ELEMENTS: With 1,880 Line Drawings of Arches, Domes, Doorways, Facades, Gables, Windows, etc., John Theodore Haneman. Sourcebook of inspiration for architects, designers, others. Bibliography. Captions. 141pp. 9 × 12. 24605-1 Pa. $7.95

BENCHLEY LOST AND FOUND, Robert Benchley. Finest humor from early 30s, about pet peeves, child psychologists, post office and others. Mostly unavailable elsewhere. 73 illustrations by Peter Arno and others. 183pp. 5⅜ × 8½. 22410-4 Pa. $4.95

ERTÉ GRAPHICS, Erté. Collection of striking color graphics: *Seasons, Alphabet, Numerals, Aces* and *Precious Stones.* 50 plates, including 4 on covers. 48pp. 9⅜ × 12¼. 23580-7 Pa. $7.95

THE JOURNAL OF HENRY D. THOREAU, edited by Bradford Torrey, F. H. Allen. Complete reprinting of 14 volumes, 1837–61, over two million words; the sourcebooks for *Walden,* etc. Definitive. All original sketches, plus 75 photographs. 1,804pp. 8½ × 12¼. 20312-3, 20313-1 Cloth., Two-vol. set $130.00

CASTLES: Their Construction and History, Sidney Toy. Traces castle development from ancient roots. Nearly 200 photographs and drawings illustrate moats, keeps, baileys, many other features. Caernarvon, Dover Castles, Hadrian's Wall, Tower of London, dozens more. 256pp. 5⅜ × 8¼. 24898-4 Pa. $6.95

AMERICAN CLIPPER SHIPS: 1833–1858, Octavius T. Howe & Frederick C. Matthews. Fully-illustrated, encyclopedic review of 352 clipper ships from the period of America's greatest maritime supremacy. Introduction. 109 halftones. 5 black-and-white line illustrations. Index. Total of 928pp. 5⅜ × 8½.
25115-2, 25116-0 Pa., Two-vol. set $17.90

TOWARDS A NEW ARCHITECTURE, Le Corbusier. Pioneering manifesto by great architect, near legendary founder of "International School." Technical and aesthetic theories, views on industry, economics, relation of form to function, "mass-production spirit," much more. Profusely illustrated. Unabridged translation of 13th French edition. Introduction by Frederick Etchells. 320pp. 6⅛ × 9¼. (Available in U.S. only)
25023-7 Pa. $8.95

THE BOOK OF KELLS, edited by Blanche Cirker. Inexpensive collection of 32 full-color, full-page plates from the greatest illuminated manuscript of the Middle Ages, painstakingly reproduced from rare facsimile edition. Publisher's Note. Captions. 32pp. 9⅜ × 12¼.
24345-1 Pa. $5.95

BEST SCIENCE FICTION STORIES OF H. G. WELLS, H. G. Wells. Full novel *The Invisible Man*, plus 17 short stories: "The Crystal Egg," "Aepyornis Island," "The Strange Orchid," etc. 303pp. 5⅜ × 8½. (Available in U.S. only)
21531-8 Pa. $6.95

AMERICAN SAILING SHIPS: Their Plans and History, Charles G. Davis. Photos, construction details of schooners, frigates, clippers, other sailcraft of 18th to early 20th centuries—plus entertaining discourse on design, rigging, nautical lore, much more. 137 black-and-white illustrations. 240pp. 6⅛ × 9¼.
24658-2 Pa. $6.95

ENTERTAINING MATHEMATICAL PUZZLES, Martin Gardner. Selection of author's favorite conundrums involving arithmetic, money, speed, etc., with lively commentary. Complete solutions. 112pp. 5⅜ × 8½.
25211-6 Pa. $3.50

THE WILL TO BELIEVE, HUMAN IMMORTALITY, William James. Two books bound together. Effect of irrational on logical, and arguments for human immortality. 402pp. 5⅜ × 8½.
20291-7 Pa. $8.95

THE HAUNTED MONASTERY and THE CHINESE MAZE MURDERS, Robert Van Gulik. 2 full novels by Van Gulik continue adventures of Judge Dee and his companions. An evil Taoist monastery, seemingly supernatural events; overgrown topiary maze that hides strange crimes. Set in 7th-century China. 27 illustrations. 328pp. 5⅜ × 8½.
23502-5 Pa. $6.95

CELEBRATED CASES OF JUDGE DEE (DEE GOONG AN), translated by Robert Van Gulik. Authentic 18th-century Chinese detective novel; Dee and associates solve three interlocked cases. Led to Van Gulik's own stories with same characters. Extensive introduction. 9 illustrations. 237pp. 5⅜ × 8½.
23337-5 Pa. $5.95

Prices subject to change without notice.

Available at your book dealer or write for free catalog to Dept. GI, Dover Publications, Inc., 31 East 2nd St., Mineola, N.Y. 11501. Dover publishes more than 175 books each year on science, elementary and advanced mathematics, biology, music, art, literary history, social sciences and other areas.